For the young Marines and their wives who will someday carry on the fine traditions of this house . . .

HOME OF THE COMMANDANTS

LEATHERNECK
ASSOCIATION
INC.
QUANTICO,
VIRGINIA

iv

HOME OF THE COMMANDANTS

by KARL SCHUON

color photographs by

LOUIS R. LOWERY

Silver wax seal ring, used by
General Henderson, is from the
Henderson-Lee collection.

JAMES L. HOPEWELL
production/art director

LOUIS R. LOWERY
photo director

RONALD D. LYONS
copy editor

HISTORY & MUSEUMS
DIVISION, HQMC
historical research

ACKNOWLEDGMENTS

For the patient, diligent research which made the original version of this book possible, the author wishes to express his sincere gratitude to LtCol David E. Schwulst, USMCR, Richard A. Long, Charles A. Wood, John Marley, Mrs. Doris Davis, Mrs. Lillian Laizure and Mr. Rowland P. Gill.

And to Albert U. Blair, Watson G. Caudill, Sara D. Jackson, William E. Lind, Jose D. Lizardo, Richard S. Maxwell and Lee D. Saegesser.

Edward J. Reese, Buford Rowland, Virginia A. Spencer and Camille Hannon.

Harry Schwartz, Thomas B. Taylor, James D. Walker. And to WO Joan Ambrose, USMC, and Charles H. Hallman.

Personnel of the Combat Pictorial Branch, Headquarters Marine Corps, particularly GySgt Thomas M. Parente, USMC, Ret.; and to personnel of the Photographic Services Section, Marine Corps Schools, Quantico, Virginia, especially, MGySgt Robert H. Mosier, USMC. And to Benjamin J. Nereck, Leatherneck photo section.

First Edition, 1966
New and Revised Edition, March, 1974

PREFACE

Square 927 in the old southeast section of Washington, D. C., has seen many changes since newly-inaugurated President Thomas Jefferson and Lieutenant Colonel Commandant William Ward Burrows first rode out on a March day in 1801 to look "for a proper place to fix the Marine Barracks on."

The Commandant's House at the north end of the square, begun by Burrows, was first occupied by his successor, Lieutenant Colonel Commandant Franklin Wharton in 1806. Since that time it has been the official residence of all succeeding Commandants of the Marine Corps and, because it was not burned during the British raid on Washington in 1814, it has good claim to being the oldest public residence in continuous use in the Nation's capital.

Each successive Commandant has left his mark, large or small, both on the shape of the Marine Corps and on the House in which he lived. Just as the Corps has changed and evolved with the years, so has the House, reflecting the life and times of its occupants, present and past.

So too has this book which is now in its second edition, reflecting as it does the extensive refurbishment of the House undertaken by General and Mrs. Robert E. Cushman, Jr.

> EDWIN H. SIMMONS
> Brigadier General, U. S. Marine Corps (Ret.)
> Director of Marine Corps History and Museums

Washington, D.C., April, 1974

Prescott cherry wood melodeon
and handmade candlesticks were
donated by BrigGen and Mrs.
Harold D. Hansen.

CONTENTS

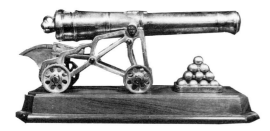

The replica of a British cannon, now in the Commandant's study, was originally presented to General Lemuel C. Shepherd, Jr., on the occasion of his first visit to Fort Henry.

HOME OF THE COMMANDANTS ...

F OR MORE THAN a century and a half, the house has cast its oblique shadows on a street only a few years older than itself. Since 1806, its yard-thick walls of brick have sheltered the home life of every United States Marine Corps Commandant. Here, in the oldest public building in continuous use in the Nation's Capital, all but the first two of the Corps' leaders have pondered the problems of their elite military organization

Here, too, the gracious first ladies of the Corps have entertained Washington society, visiting dignitaries and distinguished military leaders of other countries at charming receptions and dinners.

Now, in the Twentieth Century, the beautifully decorated house with its sparkling crystal chandeliers, mirrored fireplaces, highly polished period furniture and lush rugs has lost none of its early charm. Staircases with their balustrades, and high, arched-ceiling hallways retain a compelling timeless atmosphere, as if it were only yesterday that Commandant Archibald Henderson brought his 19-year-old bride to the house, where she remained its mistress from 1822 until her death in 1859.

There was happiness in the old house, but there was heartache, too. Beneath the deep pile carpeting, its splintered oak rafters may still remember the frustrated pacing of Commandant Anthony Gale whose unfortunate relations with a domineering Secretary of the Navy eventually led to his court-martial and dishonor.

There were days of war and decisions, too; times when the lives of thousands of Marines lay in the hands of the Corps' leaders

The house has led a full life, rich in the cherished memories of formal parties of state, squalling babies, the clatter of horses' hooves, the screech of carriage wheels, declarations of war, and pumps leaking water in the cellar.

The big things, the small things, the important events, the sentimental, family joys and sorrows, all have fused and left the

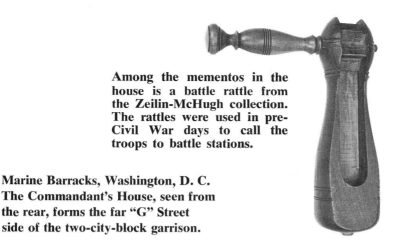

Among the mementos in the house is a battle rattle from the Zeilin-McHugh collection. The rattles were used in pre-Civil War days to call the troops to battle stations.

Marine Barracks, Washington, D. C. The Commandant's House, seen from the rear, forms the far "G" Street side of the two-city-block garrison.

house with a mellow character unequaled in American heritage.

It is perhaps ironical that the first Commandant, after the Corps' Congressional activation in 1798, Lieutenant Colonel William Ward Burrows, whose determination and skillful diplomatic persuasion resulted in the building of the house and adjoining Marine Barracks, never lived in the house. A victim of ill health, Commandant Burrows was forced to retire in 1804, nearly two years before the house was completed.

Authorization for the construction of the house and barracks—and an appropriation—came early in 1801, shortly after Thomas Jefferson had been elected to the presidency. Jefferson, a personal friend of Burrows, accompanied the Commandant on a ride through Southeast Washington in search of a site for the Marine garrison and quarters for the Commandant. An available "square" two full city blocks in area, between Eighth and Ninth Streets, and extending from "G" Street to "I" Street, was selected. Contracts were signed and building began, with Marines themselves working on the construction along with civilian laborers, carpenters and bricklayers.

Commandant Burrows' concern for adequate permanent quarters for his troops undoubtedly delayed completion of the house. But, in 1806, the Corps' third Commandant, Franklin Wharton, found that work had progressed sufficiently to enable him to move in with his wife and four sons. In the next five years, the Whartons were to become the parents of two daughters and two more sons—the first of a long roster of Commandants' children to be born in the house.

The history of the house is almost synonymous with the history of Marine Barracks, Washington, D. C., since the house, and its side buildings and wall, form the entire northern, or "G" Street, enclosure to the compound. In effect, the paneled-oak front door to the Commandant's House could have been as vulnerable a "gate" to the garrison as its main gate.

Since the architect's plans for the house never have been uncovered, it must be assumed from letters and other records that the original building was a plain two-story, brick structure with an attic. On the first floor, a main hall led to a vestibule, the dining room and a small parlor. Beyond, on the south, or barracks, side of the house were two large, formal drawing rooms. The second floor was divided into four bedrooms. Servants' quarters and storage space were provided in the attic. Meals were prepared in a kitchen situated in the basement in an area just below the dining room.

Even though the architect's yellowed plans with their faded inks may lie crumbling somewhere in the archives, the portion of the home he designed for the Commandants still stands. Additions and revisions have, however, enlarged the house and added convenient features.

The house, more than fifty years
old, was first photographed during
the Civil War. The fence separates
the garden from the parade ground.

Apparently, the house was accepted by the Commandants without major alteration for 30 years until, in 1836, requisitions were made for sums to add a veranda in the front on the "G" Street side and a cast iron fence to border the garden and separate the house from the parade ground in its huge "backyard." By this time the house also needed complete repainting. While Commandant Henderson was in Florida with half his Marine Corps, fighting the Seminoles, the work was accomplished for the tidy sum of $3,000.

Later, changes were made in the building itself. A two-story annex was built on the northeast corner. This innovation enlarged the dining room and provided room for an extra window. A butler's

pantry was added along the east side of the dining room, together with a back hall and service stairs. The second story of this annex increased the size of the bedroom above, and allowed sufficient space for a bathroom, the first and only one in the house until 1914. Another one-story addition was built on the east side of the house at a later date.

With these renovations, the house remained unchanged until 1891 when, upon the recommendation of a board of survey, appointed by Commandant Charles G. McCawley, Congress appropriated $7,550 to pay for the conversion of the attic into a practical third floor, the replacement of the old roof by the present mansard roof, and the addition of a second story to the west wing. However, Commandant McCawley was retired before the changes he had advocated could be made, and his successor, Colonel Charles Heywood, was living in the house at the time the alterations were in progress. Along with these additions, there was also a deletion; the veranda, built in 1836, was removed and the front of the house took on its present appearance. Within the house, Commandant Heywood had all of the woodwork painted brown in the belief that wood of that color would be more durable.

Until 1907, a long, narrow open porch along the south side of the house overlooked the parade ground. Brigadier General George F. Elliott, then Commandant of the Corps, ordered the porch enclosed, an act which did not entirely please some of the traditionalists who had formerly occupied the house. Along with the work on the porch, a conservatory within the north wall to the west of the house was removed and a small hothouse was erected.

By 1905, the house had changed considerably. The attic had become a third story, and a mansard roof had replaced the pointed gables.

Major General William P. Biddle became the next master of the house after the retirement of General Elliott, but apparently he found no fault with his new home and no notable renovations were made. Major General George Barnett, however, upon succeeding Biddle, immediately had the woodwork repainted from brown to white. In 1915, he also had the third floor remodeled to provide more comfortable quarters and a bath for the servants. An addition on the southeast side of the house provided a waiting room and half bath on the first floor and space for a large bathroom on the second story for the hitherto bathless master bedroom. In the same year, with the motor car firmly entrenched in the American way of life, the stable became a garage.

Personal taste and the dictates of the period had always determined the interior design of the house. Commandants and their wives pursued whatever modes of decoration they chose. Obviously, little remained after a Commandant had moved out to remind posterity that he had once lived there. Although later Commandants have followed a tradition of presenting the house with various items of historic memorabilia, it was Commandant Barnett who conceived the idea of commissioning artists to paint the portraits of each former Commandant. His purpose, although not originally to enhance the walls of the house, was twofold: the portraits would not only honor the Corps' leaders, but would record in color and detail the successive changes in the uniforms of the Marine Corps.

Appropriations, however, for the Corps were probably as difficult to come by in 1916 as they had been back in 1814 when Commandant Franklin Wharton coffered every dollar at Marine Barracks, loaded the money aboard a boat borrowed from the Navy Yard, and saved it from British hands by taking it to Georgetown, D.C., then overland to Frederick, Md., by wagon. Barnett, nevertheless, found an ally in Franklin D. Roosevelt, then Acting Secretary of the Navy, who implored the Comptroller of the Treasury to make funds available for the portraits.

"I believe," Roosevelt said, "that it is the duty of the government to encourage, in every way possible, the collection and preservation of every kind of historical material."

The persuasive Franklin Roosevelt had his way; on October 21, 1916, the Comptroller allowed the expenditure of public money for the portraits as a legitimate undertaking and, as such, the paintings would be considered permanent acquisitions in the Home of the Commandants.

Within two years, nine portraits had been commissioned. Research on the earlier Commandants was a time-consuming, painstaking process, but eventually portraits of ten Commandants were completed. Successive Commandants have had their portraits painted either by artists of their own choice, or by artists selected by their aides. The portrait of every former Commandant except one is hung in the Home of the Commandants. A likeness of the unfortunate Anthony Gale has eluded researchers with the same cunning as the architect's plans for the house in which Gale's portrait would most certainly occupy its place with the other Commandants.

Although, during the pre World War I era, many changes were made in the Marine Barracks, no major alterations were planned for the house until 1934, during the tenure of Major General John Henry Russell, Jr., the Corps' sixteenth Commandant. The large extension, built onto the house in the 1840's during Henderson's tour, had given the building an unsymmetrical appearance from the "G" Street side. In an effort to achieve balance, Commandant Russell enlarged the proportions of the dining room on the east. With this addition, the kitchen and serving facilities were moved upstairs from the basement. Under Elliott, an enclosed veranda had been erected on the south side of the house, facing the parade ground. At the same time, a sun porch had been built on top of the veranda. This second-story solarium had cut off a great deal of the light from the two south bedrooms. Under Russell, the sun porch was removed.

During the first century of the home's existence, it was only a matter of course that its interior would reflect the times. Gradually, however, in the very late 1800's and the early Twentieth Century, the house had begun to take on a "modern" look. Electric lights, new designs in furniture and draperies had begun to creep into the

The silver tray, above, is engraved with the names of all the Commandants. It was presented to the house by the officers and men of the Marine Barracks, Newport, R.I. The flat-top secretary at right was the property of BrigGen Archibald Henderson.

This original American, tilt-top, pie-crust table, circa 1820, was donated by the members of the Officers' Wives Club, of Washington, D.C.

feeling of the original house and detract from its charm. The effect became apparent to Mrs. John Russell and, determined to curb its growth, she plunged into the task of restoring the house to its original mode of decoration.

In her quest for authenticity, her research took her to Mount Vernon, the Lee Mansion in Arlington, and the early American and Victoria sections of the New York Metropolitan Museum of Art. Period experts were consulted to assure authentic colors and woods. Nor was the lighting ignored. Through Mrs. Russell's perseverance, the crystal chandeliers in the dining room and the two first-floor drawing rooms replaced the early, garish electric fixtures.

Throughout the renovations, Mrs. Russell was fortunate to have the valued, expert assistance of the wife of Marine Major General L. McCarty Little. Mrs. Little's devotion and generous help certainly influenced the results of Mrs. Russell's project. With walls, wainscoting, chandeliers and draperies establishing the mood of the early 1800's, Mrs. Russell added a number of fine period reproductions, all of which have remained in the house. Accenting these beautifully grained pieces of furniture is a pair of lacquered Regency English chairs from the period of about 1800. These were the gift of Mrs. Little to the Home of the Commandants.

A 14-piece set of cut glass, which formerly
belonged to Lieutenant Colonel John Gamble,
the first Marine officer to command a Navy
ship in combat, is displayed as a memento.

Wine glasses, once part of a set used by
BrigGen Jacob Zeilin, Seventh Comman-
dant of the Marine Corps. Donated by
John E. McHugh.

Rose Medallion dinner plates, survivors of a 77-piece dinnerware set once owned by BrigGen Jacob Zeilin.

The tradition, begun by Mrs. Little, has added numerous interesting pieces which have been presented for use in the house. Other items and furniture have been purchased by the Corps from descendants or private owners. When, in 1952, Marine Corps researchers discovered the desk once used in the house by Archibald Henderson, General Lemuel C. Shepherd, Jr., arranged for its purchase by the Corps.

The desk, in vogue in the 1840's, has a high, windowed bookcase above the writing compartment, and two hinged doors below. Henderson's descendants preserved it after his death and it was finally located in the home of Miss Katherine E. Bradley in Washington, D. C., where it came into her possession after Henderson's great granddaughter retired to a Catholic convent.

An interesting tie with the past, in regard to the desk, is a hastily scrawled note on the bottom of the middle drawer from a servant to a repairman:

"Mrs. A. Henderson Wants a Lock Put on this . . . Knob came off."

Also on display in the house are 14 pieces of cut glass, once owned by a distinguished Marine officer, Lieutenant Colonel John M. Gamble, the first Marine to command a United States man-of-war in action against the enemy. The pieces, all of the same cut, were manufactured in Ireland during the Eighteenth Century. All but one bear the initials, JMG; a serving dish, however, probably added to the set later, is initialed, ISL. The glass was a gift from Robert B. Quinby, the great grandson of John Gamble.

15

Three pieces of Rose
Medallion porcelain, a
covered tureen (above),
a tureen stand, and a
teapot (right), were
presented to the house
by Eugenia A. Lejeune.

This engraved silver cake spat-
ula, perhaps once part of a
matched set, belonged to Brig
Gen Jacob Zeilin and Mrs. Virginia Freeman Zeilin.

The round, two-level occasional
table (far right) was presented
by General Alexander Vandegrift.
The piece is a replica of the 1840's.

Replica of a book, reputed to have been carved from the wood of the frigate, "The Constitution." From the Henderson-Lee collection.

Commandant Randolph McCall Pate, whose hobby was woodworking, made the butler's table shown at right.

Along with the Gamble glass, is a three-piece set of Chinese "Rose Medallion" porcelain which was the gift of Major Eugenia A. Lejeune, USMCR, in memory of her father, Major General John Archer Lejeune, the Corps' thirteenth Commandant.

Among other interesting items of historical significance is the Taylor-Henderson Bible, which originally came into the Commandant's House when Henry Allen Taylor married Anna Henderson, the daughter of General Henderson. The couple had one son, named for his paternal grandfather and reputed to have been born in a southeast room of the home.

The memories of later Commandants are perpetuated in the house, in part, by their generous presentations of authentic pieces of furniture which have added so much to its existing beauty. A round, two-level occasional table, with spiral legs, a replica of the 1840 period, was the gift of General Alexander Archer Vandegrift, the Corps' eighteenth Commandant. Of special interest is a "butler's" coffee table, made by General Randolph McCall Pate, the Corps' twenty-first Commandant. This table, a replica of those used in Nineteenth Century English homes, has four lift leaves into which are cut handles devised for carrying the table with its beverages and food to any place in the room where guests may have gathered.

Ornamental candle holders from the Ben Hebard Fuller collection, donated by Mrs. James Ellis Jr., granddaughter of the former Commandant.

A heavy, provincial, walnut sideboard at the end of the entrance foyer was the gift of General David M. Shoup.

The visitor to the house will find, at the end of the entrance foyer, a heavy, walnut sideboard in the provincial, two-door design. This magnificent piece with its original brass pulls, was the gift of General David Monroe Shoup, the twenty-second Commandant.

A handsome mahogany desk in the Commandant's study is the gift to the house from General and Mrs. Robert E. Cushman, Jr. In Federal design, it is an exact replica of the desk used by George Washington in New York City.

These pieces will remain in the house, along with future acquisitions. Through the years, the house has been furnished with a mixture of government furniture, a few historic pieces left behind by earlier Commandants, and the personal belongings of the incumbents. With today's more modest households, it has become increasingly difficult for recent Commandants to furnish the house appropriately.

Appreciating this situation, General Robert E. Cushman, Jr., and Mrs. Cushman initiated a project shortly after he became Commandant on January 1, 1972, to correct the situation. On February 25, 1972, the Secretary of the Navy authorized the Commanding Officer, Marine Barracks, Washington, D. C., "to solicit various gifts (including contributions), devises or bequests for use in the Commandant's House."

The handsome mahogany desk in the Commandant's study is the gift to the house from General and Mrs. Robert E. Cushman, Jr.

Through the years, the old house has been renovated and enlarged, but somewhere within, its original walls still stand as monuments to the oldest landmark of the Corps.

The objective of the project has been to bring the decor and furnishings of the house to a level befitting the stature of the property and to reflect appropriately the lives and times of past Commandants. A further objective is to make the house, as a national treasure, more generally available to the Marine Corps and general public. Appropriated funds have been used and will continue to be used to maintain the house. However, government ceilings on decorating and furniture purchase do not permit the attainment of the objectives outlined. Donated funds are, therefore, a necessity.

The refurbishment has proceeded in accordance with a two-stage plan. Phase I included interior painting, covering of walls and floors, hanging of draperies and the purchase of some reproduction furniture to augment the Government furniture and historic pieces already in the house. The goal of Phase I was to establish a suitable background and setting from which to proceed to the longer-range Phase II. The objective of the second phase, which continues, is to acquire suitable period pieces and works of art, both by gift and through purchase with donated funds. While the authority for the project was obtained by the Commandant, a great deal of the responsibility for the execution of the plan has rested with Mrs. Cushman who has given unstintingly of her time and energy in pursuit of these objectives.

THE HOUSE ON "G" STREET . . .

In spring, deep-hued azaleas flank the steps leading up to the door of the Commandant's House, but like the seasons, the interior of the house has changed with each new distinguished tenant. For more than a century and a half the tastes and individualities of the Commandants and their ladies have influenced the decoration of its rooms and halls. But from era to era, beyond its modest, town house door, the visitor has found, along with its majestic drawing rooms and mirrored fireplaces, a warm, gracious cordiality.

MAIN FOYER AND CENTER HALL . . . The foyer,
left, with portraits of Commandants Biddle, Wharton, McCawley
and Lejeune, leads to a center hall with entrances to the east and
west drawing rooms.

THE DINING ROOM . . . Fine china, Chippendale chairs and a crystal chandelier are the setting for gracious dining. The china, displayed on the shelves of the cupboard, far right, once belonged to BrigGen Archibald Henderson, the Corps' fifth Commandant.

THE WEST DRAWING ROOM

THE EAST DRAWING ROOM

THE SECOND-FLOOR HALLWAY

THE SUN PORCH . . . Extending across the south side of the house, the wide porch, left, was added to the original building, enclosing the first-floor bay windows.

THE UPSTAIRS SITTING ROOM

THE COMMANDANT'S STUDY . . . Below, one of the most beautiful rooms in the house. Commandant Burrows' portrait hangs above the fireplace. At right is a painting of Commandant Shepherd.

THE BLUE ROOM . . . Above, the floral pattern in the draperies is carried over into the four-posters' bedspreads. Off-white walls accentuate the red accessories.

THE MASTER BEDROOM . . . Left, dusty rose valanced drapes and counterpane contrast with restful pale greens.

THE WRITING ROOM . . . Above, vivid blues blend with the luster of rich walnut lowboys in a setting conducive to domestic and social secretarial chores.

THE THIRD-FLOOR HALLWAY . . . At right, portraits of the Commandants surround a sofa grouping for informal tete-a-tetes.

THE THIRD-FLOOR GUEST SUITE . . . Fortunate
is the visitor who occupies these two beautiful adjoining rooms.
Soft reds are carried over from the drapes and canopied bed to
the Victorian sofa and Hepplewhite chairs. White porcelain
lamps accent the decor.

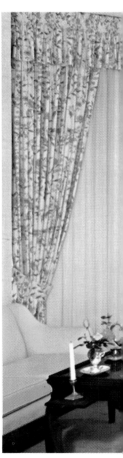

THE THIRD-FLOOR GUEST ROOMS . . . Above,
The medallion motif in the drapes and bedspread is repeated
in the upholstered chair. Right of the window is a replica of
an 1840, two-level occasional table presented by Commandant
Vandegrift.

THE GARDEN . . . On the south side of the house, separated from the parade ground by a carefully clipped hedge, is the garden. Azaleas, crepe myrtle, and other shrubs landscape the yard. There is a rose patch, bordered by petunias and forget-me-nots, a hothouse and even a small fenced vegetable garden. On warm, summer nights the huge lawn is the scene of receptions and garden parties.

MARINE BARRACKS, WASHINGTON, D. C. . . .
From the veranda of the house, overlooking the garden, Commandants, since 1806 have watched their troops and the Marine Band marching on the parade grounds. The barracks buildings, officers' quarters and the band hall have been rebuilt, but after more than one and a half centuries, the Commandant's House still stands firmly on its original foundation, still the landmark of the oldest post in the Corps.

HOME OF THE CORPS

Although the house at 801 "G" Street has been the "white house" of the Corps and the true Home of the Commandants since 1806, its back yard, two entire city blocks in Washington, D.C., served as the Home of the Corps for nearly a century. Until 1901, Headquarters Marine Corps and the offices of the Commandant were conveniently situated in a brick building only a few hundred feet, diagonally across the parade ground, from the back door of the Commandant's House.

Geographically, the location of Headquarters Marine Corps conjures up amusing visions of corporals, sergeants and young lieutenants keeping a wary eye on the Commandant's back steps in the early dawn, and hastily stubbing out cigars, placing a hot cup of coffee on the Commandant's desk, and frantically stuffing the morning editions of the *National Intelligencer* into drawers and cabinets as the back door of the house opened and their boss strode toward them, the problems of his Corps occupying a busy, alert mind. And then, in the evening, it is not difficult to visualize him, stepping briskly across the clipped parade ground grass, in anticipation of a cool mint julep on his veranda and chuckling over the victories he may have won that day with the Federal Government in appropriations, recruiting allowances and pay raises for his men.

But, there were many days during that first century when some of the Commandants may have climbed those back steps with weary, frustrated frowns—days of war, when the Corps' leaders searched their brains for ways to meet the demands for Marine detachments from their tiny Corps to serve on shore stations and in ships, sailing the oceans half a world away.

Here, too, the early Commandants awakened to the raucous calls of cadence in their back yard as drill instructors harangued recruits for 105 years until, in 1911, a recruit depot was established at Parris Island. It is also possible that many a Commandant's wife closed the south windows of the house to muffle the discordant wailings of an infant band rehearsing itself into eventual excellence and world fame—a band which grew to manhood without ever leaving its home at Marine Barracks, Washington, except for concert tours and ceremonials.

Training for the enlisted men, as well as for the young officers, in the back yard, under the Commandant's closest scrutiny, built an efficient Corps, but it is doubtful whether some of the Commandants' wives, with newborn, sleeping babies, appreciated the thunder of the two artillery pieces their husbands were using nearby to train their cannoneers.

And, through it all, since 1806, the old house has stood, looking southward over its master's garrison in the Nation's Capital, reveling in the stalwart leadership of its distinguished tenants, warm in a cordiality tempered with many vintage years, proud of its birthright as the house at the Home of the Corps.

But, the birth of the house was synonymous with the birth of Marine Barracks, Eighth & Eye Streets, S.E.

In the year 1800, the newly activated Marine Corps, only two years old, was headquartered in the City of Philadelphia, then the seat of the U. S. Government. Ten years earlier, a site on the Potomac River, "not to exceed 10 square miles," had been chosen for the new capital city. Federal agencies awaited word to move south to their permanent offices in the "City of Washington." On May 15, 1800, the word came. Earlier, in April, Congress had authorized President John Adams to move the executive department of the government to the newly-built city, one of the few in the history of the world to be planned as a national capital. Shortly thereafter, Federal records and 137 clerks were moved from Philadelphia to Washington. The transition had begun.

Evidently, the office of the Secretary of the Navy lost no time in establishing itself in the new capital, for on June 23, 1800,

Secretary of the Navy Benjamin Stoddert wrote to Lieutenant Colonel Commandant William Ward Burrows from his office in one of the "Six Buildings" on Pennsylvania Avenue, alerting him on the Corps' move to the capital.

"Sir," the Secretary wrote, "I have had so many things to attend to since my arrival here, that I have scarcely been able to think about the Marines. Capt. Tingey (Superintendent of the Washington Navy Yard) pointed out some houses to me this morning, which I think will very well answer for Barracks—and he seems to have no doubt that you can be well accommodated also.

"A thousand reasons plead for your being at once in the City instead of stopping at Bladensburg. The place languishes for want of a little spirit of Exertion. Upon the whole, I think you had better hold yourself in readiness to leave Phila. with all your dependencies in a few days—but not to move until you hear again from me. . . ."

On June 26, 1800, Commandant Burrows answered:

"I only await your orders and shall repair immediately to any place you shall direct.

"When I receive yr. orders, I shall lose no time in removing myself & Dependencies, and shall use every Exertion when there, to promote the City of Washington.

I have the Honor to be
with great Respect
Yr. Obedt Sert
WWB
Lt, C.C.
M.C."

The order for the Corps to move to Washington came, and a letter from the Commandant to the Secretary, dated July 3, 1800, stated:

"I shall immediately hire a vessel and send my mens Furniture etc. off by Wednesday next. My Quarter-Master shall be ordered on, to determine if possible (a suitable) spot in the City. . . .

"I am much obliged by your polite offer of your house, which I shall accept, if I cannot be otherwise accommodated . . . but I

WILLIAM WARD BURROWS
Second Commandant

care not for myself where my House is, so as I can get my men comfortably provided for."

In the same letter, the Commandant made an early plea for a Marine Barracks:

"I wish," he wrote, "when you have leisure you will take into Consideration the building of at least one wing of Buildings for Barracks. It will save money to the Publick, and be more comfortable to us. . . ."

Commandant Burrows and his staff arrived in the Federal City on July 15, 1800, and moved into a private house in Georgetown where they established their headquarters. The house also provided living accommodations for the Commandant and his staff.

Then, aboard ship, by stage and on foot, the first Marines began to pour into Washington, and the tents of the first contingent dotted the slope of Prospect Hill on the Georgetown side of Rock Creek. The arrival of a vessel with additional men and equipment, however, made a larger camp site necessary. Camp Hill, or Peter Hill, near "E" Street between 23rd and 25th Streets, N.W., was designated as the new Marine encampment, and before long, residents of the new capital were being shaken from their slumbers by reveille.

Although Commandant Burrows expressed dissatisfaction with the temporary headquarters arrangements, the troops during the summer months were comfortable in their *al-fresco* accommodations. In fact, the Commandant, in a letter to Captain Franklin Wharton, who had remained in Philadelphia where he commanded the Marine Barracks, stated enthusiastically:

"... I wish we had the pleasure of your Company for one Day in Camp, that you might view our beautiful Situation. It is delightful & Charming, and every Ones Curiosity is excited to visit us."

The summer, however, grew into a lethargic fall. Commandant Burrows, in order to relieve the monotony of his troops, organized what was undoubtedly the first USO-type party for Marines in the Nation's Capital. Burrows, unable to attend the wedding of a friend's ward in Philadelphia, decided to hold a party for his men in her honor. A letter to the friend, written the day following the party, provides all the details and leaves little doubt that the "ball" could not have been more successful, despite a few of the Commandant's bitter complaints.

The letter is headed "Camp, City of Washington, Octbr. 2nd 1800."

"As I could not, my dear friend, be at the wedding last evening, I resolved to give a Ball the same Night at my Camp, in compliments to yr. Ward. I invited every young lady in Geo. Town & some from elsewhere. All would have come, but for the Interference of Mothers & some such powerful People prevented one or two. We had not the pleasure of the Johnson's because Mr. J had invited a Lady from Chas.ton to Tea who I had also invited: her Engagement was first, and she would not put it off, saying She had no idea of giving way to Chits [pert, saucy girls] so 2 or 3 solemn Characters went and scalded their Mouths with her Tea, whilst about 60 of us were enjoying the finest night I ever saw. The Evening was mild, The Moon divine, & the Music the best I ever heard; made up of Wilkinson's and my Band.

"We gave the usual Refreshments to the ladies in the early Part of the Evening after which a cold Collation [a buffet, snacks] which the Gentlemen seemed to admire, being ornamented with some of B. W. Morris's best. The Ladies retired about 12, but the young Men kept it up till day light in serenading etc. . . . The

Situation of our Encampment is immensely beautiful, and tho' Night, yet the view of the Potomack was solemnly great from the reflection of the Moon . . ."

But, Burrows, recognizing the fact that Washington, D. C., winters can be as bitter as the summers are sweet, sent a succinct note to Captain Wharton on November 13th, 1800.

"We went into Barracks on the 11th Instant and well we did, for it has been blustering Weather since."

The "Barracks" were buildings rented from the War Department. The Commandant, however, seeking permanent accommodations for a sizeable body of troops and their officers, together with office facilities necessary for a headquarters operation, persisted in his requests to Congress for appropriations to build them.

On March 6, 1801, two days after Thomas Jefferson had succeeded John Adams in the Presidency, the Secretary of the Navy wrote Burrows, informing him that $20,000 had been appropriated for the erection of a Marine Barracks in Washington.

"The earlier their erection is commenced," Stoddert wrote, "the sooner will the public be relieved from the expence of House rent; and, I presume, with the aid of Mechanics & others of your Marines, that Barracks may be erected for twenty thousand dollars, which without such aid, would cost 50000.

"Having no predilection for any particular spot of ground, I leave that point to be determined by yourself. . . ."

However, Commandant Burrows was not left to roam the new district in solitude, searching for a home for his Marines; Jefferson, a personal friend of the Commandant, and deeply interested in the welfare of the Corps, accompanied Burrows. On March 31, 1801,

the Commandant wrote to Captain Wharton in Philadelphia:

"... I have been all this morning engaged riding with the President looking out for a proper place to fix the Marine Barracks on. It is not yet absolutely determined, but I have no doubt it will be fixed at the Navy Yard. ..."

The Commandant's ride with Jefferson covered the entire area in the lower, southeastern section of Washington in which the Navy Yard was situated. The original plan for the city placed the Capitol Building in the center of the district. North Capitol Street, extending due north of the Capitol, and South Capitol Street, running due south of the site, were designated as the north and south axis. East Capitol Street, extending due east of the Capitol, and The Mall, a broad park extending westward to the Potomac River, became the east and west axis. Streets to the north of the east-west axis were given the letters of the alphabet; those to the south were similarly called "A", "B", "C", etc. Streets to the east and west of the north-south axis were given numbers, thus there is a 1st Street on each side of the Capitol building. The fact that Washington, D. C., remains "quartered" today accounts for the somewhat bothersome and bewildering initials, S.W., S.E., N.W. and N.E. which follow street addresses.

The President had expressed a desire that the Barracks be located near the Navy Yard and within easy marching distance of the Capitol. The available "City block" lying between Eighth and Ninth Streets, S.E., and "G" and "I" Streets, seemed an ideal location. The letter "I" is sometimes spelled phonetically, thus "I" becomes "Eye." The tract, on the surveyor's map, was called simply "Square Number 927." In June of 1801, the President authorized its purchase for the building of a "permanent military garrison at the seat of the government."

Thomas Jefferson and Commandant Burrows rode through the new Washington area in search of a site for the Marine Barracks.

The cost of the Square had been estimated at about $4,000, but evidently the importance of the purchaser raised the price to $6,247.18. The tract measured 250 feet east and west, and 615 feet north and south. Its dimensions have never changed. The final price for the city block brought its cost up to about four cents per square foot.

With the purchase of the land, construction began as soon as contracts for the materials and work had been negotiated. Commandant Burrows accepted the suggestion of the Secretary of the Navy that Marine mechanics and craftsmen be used in the erection of the Barracks, and Military Occupational Specialties of the day were hastily tallied on a Table of Organization which would give the project an additional construction crew headed by civilian and military bosses. Burrows, engrossed with the urgent need to have his men not only comfortably provided for, but stationed in a formidable permanent military garrison as a force in readiness, expedited the work on the Barracks, attaching less importance to the construction of his own residence. Undoubtedly, his zeal to complete the quarters for his men in as short a time as possible accounts for the fact that he was the only Commandant, aside from Samuel Nicholas, who did not enjoy the pleasure of living in the house.

Ill health forced him to tender his resignation on February 23, 1804, and it was accepted by the Secretary of the Navy on March

7, 1804. At that time the southern wing of the Barracks and the Center House officers' quarters had been completed, and work on the Commandant's House was well under way.

Although the years 1801 to 1805 were filled with busy construction on Square 927, they were also beset with heated arguments about contracts and bids, bothersome haggling over the amounts of materials used and outright unacceptable construction. Benjamin Henry Latrobe, then Surveyor of the Public Buildings of the United States, also supervising building for the Navy Department,, appears to have handled most of the contracts and finances on the Barracks construction. That he was ever watchful of economy is evidenced in some blunt correspondence over the number of bricks used in the Commandant's House. The contractor had charged the government for 245,000 bricks, but Latrobe, a leading architect of the time, sharpened his pencil and from available measurements of the house, came up with his own figure—225,000 bricks. However, following letters revealed that there may have been a misunderstanding about the actual measurements. The exact number of bricks in the Commandant's House may never have been determined, but the incident demonstrates clearly Latrobe's cost-conscious vigilance.

In addition to the number of bricks, strong objections were made regarding their quality. However, the construction continued, despite the discord between Latrobe and the contractors. Eventually, the quality of workmanship, done by civilians, became so inferior that the Commandant appealed to the Secretary of the Navy for an appraisement of the construction. A board was convened and the report on their survey recommended that the Barracks should not be "received" from the contractors until the South Wing and the Center House were improved by "such demolitions or repairs" as were needed. The north wing was to be razed and the walls and stone foundations rebuilt.

Additional appropriations, during the years 1803 to 1806, totaled $11,076.65. This sum made possible the completion of the Commandant's House and a magazine. The armory was enlarged and the condemned north wing was rebuilt.

FRANKLIN WHARTON
Third Commandant

With the resignation of William Ward Burrows as Commandant in 1804, Captain Franklin Wharton, senior officer in the Corps, was immediately appointed Lieutenant Colonel Commandant. Wharton, a man of considerable means, lost no opportunity to spend his money in the interest of his Corps. He felt a strong sense of social responsibility and entertained on a large scale, not only for his brother officers, but for distinguished personages from every avenue of government and culture, whose close friendships he had developed over the years.

Little wonder, then, that under Commandant Wharton's eager desire for an official residence where his social functions would become small military affairs of state, work on the house progressed rapidly. However, the Northern Wing of the Barracks also received its share of attention.

Although civilian contractors had been blamed and reprimanded for unacceptable construction, Marines were still being utilized as laborers, mechanics and carpenters. Wharton, in a gesture of "indulgence" toward them, exempted them from military duties and issued an additional gill of rum, daily, to each man. The rum may have been an incentive, for it appears that both the Barracks and the house were completed in late 1805 or early 1806.

In spite of relentless research and probing into the unfathomable archives of the Nation's Capital, the original plans for neither the barracks nor the Commandant's House have been found, but other documents clearly name George Hadfield, an Italian-born, English architect, as the designer of the Marine Barracks.

However, an advertisement in the *National Intelligencer,* on April 3, 1801, offered "a premium of 100 dollars . . . to any person who will exhibit the best plan of barracks for the Marines, sufficient to hold 500 men, with their officers, and a house for the Commandant." It must therefore be presumed that whoever designed the Barracks, would also have been the architect for the Commandant's House.

The fact that a Lieutenant Colonel Anne Louis de Tousard, who had served in the American Revolution, obviously responded to the advertisement on May 8, 1801, diverted researchers for a number of years. Tousard had actually submitted "a very eligant plan of the Barracks for the Marine Corps," to President Jefferson via the Navy Department. No trace of Tousard's plan has ever been found, but later research has turned up absolute evidence that George Hadfield had not only designed the Barracks, but was paid for his work.

In 1795, Hadfield had been recommended by the American artist, John Trumbull, to the Commissioners of the City of Washington for the position of Superintendent of the Capitol, then being constructed. After his acceptance, his commissions were the original Treasury Building and the Executive Offices, both burned by the British in 1814. Hadfield also designed the County Jail and City Hall of Washington, the Arsenal on Greenleaf's Point, the Van Ness Mausoleum in Oak Hill Cemetery and the Custis-Lee Mansion in Arlington which overlooks the Lincoln Memorial and the Potomac River.

His pen and ink sketch, which accompanies this text, was discovered in 1965, in the Records of the Treasury Department, and shows, "a Guard, or Officer's House, in the Center of the range of Barracks agreeably to the aforesaid plan, altered by Capt. Stevenson." With it were specifications for the contractors, listed as Bill of Particulars No. 1 and No. 2 "to finish in a complete workmanlike manner a range of Barracks with the Arcade, etc. agreeably to the approved plan of Mr. Hadfield lodged at the Navy Office. . ."

The plan depicts the original Center House which was destroyed by fire in 1829. Unfortunately, Hadfield's complete plans for the Barracks and "house for the Commandant" have not yet been found.

George Hadfield's claim to the title of architect of the Barracks and Commandant's House is further strengthened by the record of the issue of Warrant Number 871 on the U.S. Treasury, dated May 20, 1801, for the payment of $100 to him "for plan of Marine Barracks." On December 31, 1801, an additional Warrant granted

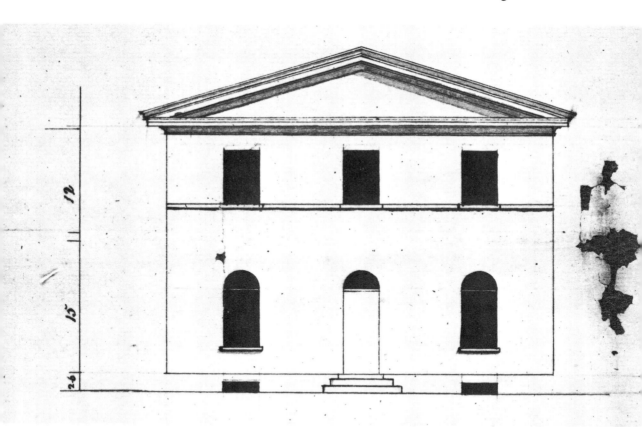

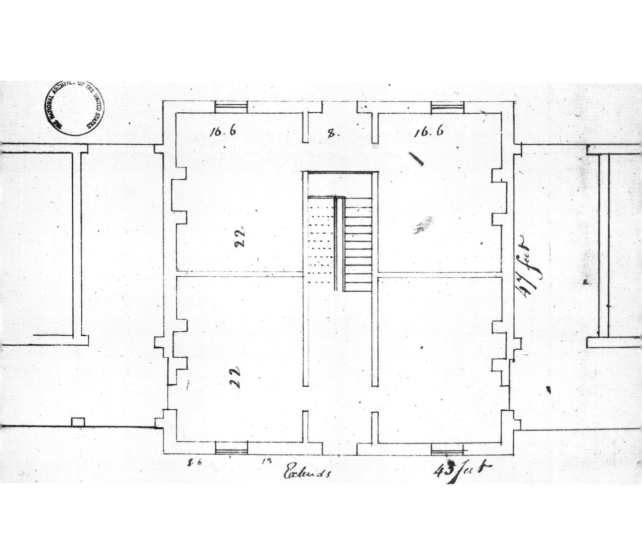

16.6   8.   16.6

22.

22.

8.6   19   Extends   43 feet

43 feet

him $60 "for drawing an elevation plan of barracks, etc."

It is notable that a prominent architectural author, commenting on plans for a naval hospital in 1812, to have been designed by Benjamin Latrobe, and built near the Barracks, complimented Hadfield.

"It" [the naval hospital] he wrote, "would have produced a building, both useful and beautiful, and together with Hadfield's marine barracks and the Navy Yard gate nearby, would have created a handsome naval center."

Although Hadfield had reached unforeseen pinnacles of architectural fame, Latrobe wrote of him:

"He loiters here, ruined in fortune, temper and reputation, nor will his irritable pride and neglected study ever permit him to take the station in the art which his elegant taste and excellent talent ought to have obtained."

At the age of 62, George Hadfield died in Washington, D.C., on February 5, 1826. Continued research may eventually establish him without a doubt as the architect of the Commandant's House. But, until that day, it must be assumed that his contract to design the Barracks also included the plans for the Commandant's Quarters.

The house, with its front entrance on "G" Street, gave the Commandant a full view of the entire Barracks quadrangle from the rear windows which framed the parade grounds. The original building had two stories and an attic with dormer windows under a hipped roof. The main floor was divided into two large formal drawing rooms on the south, or Barracks, side of the house. Across the front, or "G" Street side, were a main hall, a vestibule and two smaller rooms. The room toward the east was used as a dining room and was served from the basement. There were four bedrooms on the second floor, two facing the parade ground and two others in the front of the house. The attic provided space for servants' quarters and storage.

With the Barracks completed, Commandant Wharton could see, from his bedroom window, looking south, a small stable for his horses in the extreme northeast corner to his left and, to the east, there was a building which billeted the officers of the Barracks and accommodated the offices of Headquarters Marine Corps. Beside this building were a stable, the commissary storeroom and a shed with water closets and bathing facilities.

On his right, to the west and midway down the boundary of the parade ground, stood the Center House, quarters for the junior officers. One-story brick buildings flanked the Center House, separated from it by eight feet. The northernmost building contained the billiard room, barber shop, bakery, dining room and kitchen. The south building was used as sleeping quarters for the guard, a guard room and prison. A small house in the southeast corner contained a swimming pool. The Barracks were enclosed by a stone wall, two feet thick and eight to ten feet high, with the main entrance located on the south side of the Center House

That the Whartons entertained extensively has been well established, but, in addition, there can be little doubt that the Commandant's House bustled with family life. Franklin Wharton had married Mary Clifton in Christ Church, Philadelphia, on October 1, 1800. By the time the couple moved into the house they were already the parents of four children: Clifton, born October 22, 1801; George Washington, born May 12, 1803; Franklin, born June 3, 1804; and William Lewis, born December 17, 1805. Four more children were yet to be born while the Whartons lived there. The first two births were girls, Ellen Clifton, born May 18, 1807, and Ana Maria, born August 22, 1809. Two more sons, Alfred, born June 1, 1810, and Henry Williams, born September 27, 1811, completed the family portrait.

Simultaneously, with Wharton's occupancy of the fresh, new, sparkling Home of the Commandant, came the termination of the war with the Barbary pirates. Since practically the entire Navy had been involved in this conflict with the Barbary States extending along the northern coast of Africa, Wharton's responsibility had been to provide Marine detachments for the increasing number of vessels leaving American shores. Now, with favorable treaties, which had brought peace, Congress turned its attention to rigid economy. As the ships returned from the war zones, they were

65

either decommissioned or their crews greatly reduced. The Corps, too, suffered. By December 2, 1807, its actual strength was down to 26 officers and 722 enlisted Marines. Commandant Wharton, like his predecessor, was having a difficult time meeting the requirements for Marines to man the seven shore stations, in addition to providing detachments for the remaining ships of the Navy.

This aggravating situation may have accounted for the somewhat indifferent attitude Wharton had acquired toward the Marine Band, well established at the Barracks under the fond pampering of Commandant Burrows and President Thomas Jefferson.

Although the Act of Congress, establishing the new Corps in 1798, specifically mentioned the inclusion of "32 fifers and drummers," it gave Burrows no authority to organize a band, nor to finance it with Corps funds. These formidable obstacles might well have deterred a less aggressive music lover than the Commandant, but he plunged ahead, organizing a band of sorts in Philadelphia, even before the Corps' move to Washington. On July 17, 1800, the band packed its instruments and followed the troops to the Capital. With no government aid available, Burrows had simply established a "Band Fund" by unofficially "suggesting" that all officers should contribute a small amount from their pay each month. The officers complied, some willingly, others after reprimands from their Commandant if they were delinquent.

With the Band's coffers growing and an opportunity to build its popularity with Washington concerts, Burrows immediately ordered new instruments. In a letter to Lieutenant Edward Hall, in Philadelphia, on August 31, 1800, the Commandant wrote:

"Procure and send with all convenient dispatch the articles hereafter mentioned. . .

"2 French Horns. 2 C. Clarinets, 1 Bassoon

"1 Bass Drum, 2 feet & ½ long and 2 feet in diameter.

"Let some reeds be sent for the Clarinets, and Bassoon."

Evidently, Burrows didn't trust Hall's knowledge of horns and drums, for he added:

"You must endeavor to have them selected by a judge of musical instruments."

On October 3rd, the impatient Commandant again wrote to Hall. "You must keep a steady lookout," he urged, "for an opportunity to send the Musical instruments to Geo. Town, City of Washington or Alexandria—any of these places are all one & the same thing."

The instruments finally arrived and the Band achieved notable popularity both in its concerts for the President and for appearances before the public. By 1803, however, the demands on the Marine Band—the only military band in the city—had become so numerous that only half could be filled. President Jefferson, another lover of fine music, suggested that Burrows make an effort to enlist musicians in Italy, since that country seemed to have a margin on musical talent, and bring them to the Washington Barracks as Marines, thus giving the Capital two "national" bands—one American, the other Italian.

Commandant Burrows was delighted to comply and he sent word immediately to a Captain John Hall, then about to board ship for the Mediterranean, and ordered him to recruit some Italian musicians who would be used in the formation of a second Marine Band. Captain Hall viewed his assignment seriously, but several years passed before Hall was able to complete the roster of Italian Marine musicians. Meanwhile, ill health had forced the retirement of Commandant Burrows and Franklin Wharton had been appointed to the office.

Apparently, Burrows had neglected to mention his Italian imports to Wharton, who went into a rage when he received a letter dated February 28, 1805, from Captain Hall informing him that Marine Barracks, Washington, could prepare to receive the 18 Italian musicians he had enlisted—and their wives and children.

Wharton's consternation is understandable. With shore installations and ships' detachments to be filled, the last thing he needed was a contingent of temperamental foreign musicians, none of whom even spoke the English language. Adding further to the Commandant's ire was the fact that one of the Italian "recruits" was nine years old, two were ten years of age, and a fourth lad had just reached his 12th birthday. Nor was Wharton happy with the financial arrangements made by Captain Hall; "I have been obliged,"

Hall wrote, "to give the Leader 50 Dolls. and the rest 10 Dollars Bounty, with a ration to 8 of their wives." Unaware that he was heaping Wharton's displeasure on his head, Hall had also spent a fortune on fine musical instruments.

Since the entire troupe, including the wives and children, had been put aboard the Frigate *Chesapeake* which was still in the Mediterranean, Wharton delayed his reply to Captain Hall until June 29, 1805.

"I have received your letter from Palermo . . ." Wharton wrote. "That part of it which relates to a band of music, I cannot comprehend. You observe the Commandant had ordered a band procured, it, of course, belongs to the ship. He could not order it for the Corps. You then remark that you have engaged it for the Marine Corps, under the usual enlistment. This must be equally incorrect. I have never given any orders for the collection of a band in the Mediterranean and it will not be mentioned as belonging to the Corps. The expenses already arising from this engagement, I find enormous, by bounty and purchase of instruments, and I am well assured will not be paid. The Secretary of the Navy can never consent to allow two Military Bands for one Corps, and the private fund (Burrows' officer donations) hitherto used, has been done away."

Wharton's scathing letter apparently never reached Hall, for in September 1805, when Hall's ship reached Hampton Roads, Va., he informed the Commandant by letter that he had "added 18 good musicians to his detachment" and that he hoped Colonel Wharton would be pleased with them. The ship then proceeded up the Potomac to Washington.

On September 19, 1805, Gaetano Carusi, the Leader of the Italian Band, wrote that he and his musicians had "arrived in a desert, in fact, a place containing some two or three taverns, with a few scattered cottages or log huts, called the City of Washington. . ."

The unfortunate Captain Hall was severely reprimanded at Headquarters Marine Corps and asked to explain his actions. Wharton, satisfied that an embarrassing situation existed, called a hasty meeting with the Secretary of the Navy, but the only conclusion that could be reached resulted in an order, grudgingly given by the Commandant, that the "Italian Band" would "live in quarters within the garrison . . . and be under the same regulations as the Old Band is and has been. . ." By August 15th the Italian musicians had either been discharged or absorbed into the regular Marine Band.

Under Wharton, the Corps' strength grew slowly, but not rapidly enough to face the war in the offing with Great Britain. On June 18, 1812, when Congress officially declared war on England, the Corps numbered only 1,869 officers and men.

In spite of the fact that a state of war existed, the Corps was held at its same strength for the first two years of the conflict. Nevertheless, the Commandant was again expected to furnish detachments for a Navy, growing faster than the limited Corps. The demand, at one time, was so great that the ranks in the squadrons of Perry on Lake Erie and MacDonough on Lake Champlain had to be augmented by soldiers. It is, however, evident that Wharton distributed his tiny Corps skillfully, since a documented chronology of the Marine Corps from 1812 to 1814 lists more than a hundred naval engagements in which Marines participated.

But the year 1814 might well have brought annihilation, rather than considerable damage, to the Nation's newly built capital and the Marine Barracks. Wharton, himself, may have viewed the year dimly as he reminisced during his remaining tour as Commandant.

Although engagements at sea had taxed the extended efforts of the U. S. Navy up to 1814, Great Britain had been unable to devote her full attention to the war with the States, having been somewhat preoccupied by her struggle with Napoleon. Now, in 1814, with the French Emperor disposed of, for the moment, she was able to withdraw her veteran troops from Europe and send them to the American theater of operations. In spring, several thousand of the Duke of Wellington's Peninsular veterans were embarked aboard transports bound for Bermuda. Here an advance base was set up. Target: America.

On August 17th, the British fleet entered Chesapeake Bay and easily drove their opposition, Commodore Joshua Barney's small flotilla of gunboats, up the Patuxent River. On the 20th, the British landed their troops at the town of Benedict on the west bank of the Patuxent. With an attack on Washington imminent, Barney destroyed his gunboats, salvaged the naval guns, and with his crews, headed for Washington.

On his arrival he was joined by troops from the Marine Barracks which numbered 103 officers and men under Captain Samuel Miller, Adjutant of the Corps. Now, with a force of about 500 men, Barney marched out of the Capital to join the troops of Brigadier General George Winder, in overall command of the defense of Washington. Winder set up his lines at Bladensburg, Md., only a short distance from Washington's northeastern boundary, on the morning of August 24th. At noon, the British attack came. Winder's troops, most of them poorly trained militia and volunteers, were no match for the 3,000 veteran soldiers of the enemy. Three times, however, the Marines and Sailors repulsed the British after they had broken through the American lines, but Barney's small force was left exposed when the Redcoats swept around both American flanks in a double envelopment. Winder's troops fled in a panic-stricken rout. The Sailors and Marines, in danger of being surrounded, were forced to withdraw, leaving their wounded, including Barney and Miller. Major General Robert Ross, commanding the British, was so impressed by the valiant stand taken by the Marines that, in respect, he had the wounded Americans cared for in a field hospital set up at Bladensburg, and left them there to be returned to friendly hands after he had withdrawn from the town. The surviving Marines, now under Captain Alexander Sevier, went on to Baltimore to assist in the defense of that city. The troops, however, left Baltimore before the British attack.

Unopposed, the British marched into Washington, prepared to demand the surrender of the Capital. They were somewhat surprised to find that neither the President, the Cabinet, nor the members of Congress were at home. Neither was the Commandant of the Marine Corps. Alone with their prize, except for a trembling public, the British went about burning as many public buildings as they could identify. They set fire to the Capitol, the White House—

then called the Presidential Mansion—the Treasury, War Office, Arsenal, the Library of Congress and others. The Marine Barracks and Commandant's House were spared.

Many theories have been offered to explain why General Ross did not destroy the Barracks and House, but none has ever been proved. There have been those who contended that Ross and the Admiral of the fleet intended to use the house for their headquarters, but in their hasty withdrawal the next day they neglected to set fire to it. Other theories insist that the courage and fighting spirit of the Marines at Bladensburg left General Ross with so much admiration that he couldn't bring himself to burn the garrison.

A more likely explanation has grown from the fact that residents in the neighborhood at 8th and "I" Streets pleaded with the General not to burn the Barracks, since it would endanger their adjoining private property.

The Commandant's absence from the Capital while the British were ravaging its buildings was explained in one of Wharton's subsequent reports.

"I was," he said simply, "at Fredericktown with the paymaster."

This was an absolute truth, since Wharton, at the approach of the British, had loaded the payroll and various documents aboard a boat he had borrowed from the Navy Yard and, with the paymaster, made his way to Frederick, Md., by way of Georgetown, D.C. Under the circumstances, it seemed appropriate that the Commandant should follow suit when all the other high officials of the government had evacuated the Capital when it appeared that Washington was defenseless. It is doubtful whether the Commandant could have stood off the entire British army by himself, with perhaps a few cooks, elderly orderlies and boy field musics to help him, but jibes from the other services and an indignant outcry from a young Marine captain named Archibald Henderson, eventually forced a court-martial at which Commandant Wharton was completely exonerated for his action at the time of the British invasion.

In spite of the fact that Wharton had actually taken the payroll and everything else of value to Frederick, a legend of buried treasure was born at the Barracks. The saga concerns two sergeants who were supposedly detailed to bury a chest containing Marine Corps funds somewhere in the vicinity of the compound. Early figures started at $2,500 in cash which was kept on hand for "contingent" expenses. But, as the legend grew, the amount grew with it, often exceeding the preposterous sum of $50,000.

Versions of the legend differ; one story states positively that the two men, after burying the chest, joined their comrades at Bladensburg and died in action, taking to their graves the secret of the treasure.

That the Capital suffered, even though the Barracks and Commandant's House did not, is reflected in a letter from Wharton to Captain John Heath at Sackets Harbor, New York.

"Before this," the Commandant wrote, "you will have heard of the strange events of our last two weeks in which so much has been done, & so much suffered by our city, that really all appears like a dream unless we pass through the streets & avenues & behold the sad effects which but these two weeks have produced—We stand safe at Barracks except what was done by the violence of a Tornado or storm, which carried all before it—The Navy Yard, with all the

shops & Vessels were destroyed . . . Our troops have suffered much
—Captain Miller & Sevier with Lieut Nicoll were wounded, the
former in the arm badly, but I hope all are mending . . ."

Vandalism, always the by-product of catastrophy, was rampant
and the Barracks evidently received its share. However, it wasn't
until about six weeks after the British attack that the Quartermaster,
in well-couched language, discreetly put out the word:

"Those persons who took any books or property belonging to
the Corps for safekeeping with a view of returning them, will please
send them to the Quarter Master's Office. . . . Those who are known
to have property belonging to the Marine Corps in their possession
. . . will be waited upon by an officer of justice in a few days, if the
property be not immediately returned."

The war with England ended in December with the signing of a
treaty at Ghent, and Marines at the Barracks returned to their
normal peacetime duties. Under Wharton, uniforms and equipment were standardized and military practices became more regular
throughout the Corps. By 1817, however, the Commandant was
leading a Corps which had been cut to half its wartime strength.
On March 3, 1817, Congress had passed the Peace Establishment
Act which had set the limit of the Marine Corps at 50 officers and
942 enlisted. Standards, quite likely, were higher in this smaller
Corps, and with little action other than a few skirmishes with
pirates, Wharton rested easily with few Marine commitments to be
met.

At the Barracks, an innovation had been introduced which may
well have been the forerunner of today's enlisted clubs. One of the
neighborhood saloons had been selected for the Marines' exclusive
use! An act, approved by the City of Washington on October 9,
1817, had made it official. The act read, in part:

"Whereas it hath been represented . . . that it hath been customary for the Marines stationed in this City . . . to have liberty to
visit one particular house or shop for refreshment, which hath been
sanctioned by the officers of the said Marine Corps; that no other
person visit the said house or shop . . . and that the peace and quiet
of the neighborhood is greatly promoted by such arrangement;

Therefore, Be it enacted . . . that the Mayor be . . . authorized to license such persons as the Commanding Officer of the Marine Corps shall from time to time recommend as a shopkeeper, to retail liquors to the Marines stationed in the City of Washington . . ."

Whether this act was exactly complimentary to the Marines is a matter of conjecture. One note of consolation, however, is the fact that the act did not exclude the Marines from drinking in any of the other public taverns in the neighborhood.

The death of Lieutenant Colonel Franklin Wharton in office on September 1, 1818, created a problem for the Administration since the next senior officer in the Corps, Major Anthony Gale, appeared to lack the qualifications and character which would be expected of a Commandant of the Marine Corps. Unfavorable opinions of his professional competence and a past record of misconduct, whether justified or not, seemed to indicate that Gale would be an unwise choice. However, military tradition of the day dictated seniority. After a delay of six months, during which Major Archibald Henderson took over as acting Commandant, seniority triumphed and, with the grudging concurrence of the Secretary of the Navy, Anthony Gale was promoted to Lieutenant Colonel and named the fourth Commandant of the Corps on March 3, 1819.

Gale's tenure was neither effective nor happy, due in great measure to the constant meddling of the Secretary of the Navy, Smith Thompson. Gale's orders were continually countermanded by the Secretary whose arbitrary actions appeared to usurp the Commandant's authority. On one occasion, Gale had ordered one of his officers to a new duty station, whereupon the Secretary immediately revoked Gale's order and gave the officer eight months' leave. Ironically, a few months before, the Secretary had sent Gale a terse directive in which he had instructed the Commandant to grant no more than 60 days' leave to his officers, regardless of circumstances. Since Gale's difficulties with the Secretary were well known to his officers, his problems became the subjects of countless cruel jibes, in which many of his officers flaunted their influence with the Secretary over Gale's authority.

With his patience and pride taxed beyond endurance, Gale wrote

an official letter in which he attempted to analyze the divisions of authority and function between his command and the Office of the Secretary of the Navy. Having filed his complaint, Gale began drinking and three weeks later, he was placed under arrest for ". . . being intoxicated in common dram shops and other places of low repute in the City of Washington . . ."

At his court-martial, Gale pleaded temporary insanity and asked permission to introduce defense witnesses to support his plea. Permission, he was informed, would have to come from the Secretary of the Navy, since the Secretary had ordered his arrest. In answer, the Secretary simply stated that the court was competent to handle such matters. Although the records of the court-martial exist, they contain no mention of these witnesses.

On September 18, 1820, Anthony Gale was found guilty as charged and sentenced "to be cashiered" from the service. President James Monroe approved the sentence in October. Shortly thereafter, armed with a copy of the court-martial proceedings, Gale began a 15-year struggle to establish his case of temporary mental derangement. In 1835 he was awarded a stipend of $15 a month, later increased to $25 a month, which he received until his death in 1843. Few records survive the man who spent only 19 long, unhappy months as the master of the Home of the Commandants. Historians have, on many occasions, dismissed his services to the Corps as "negligible," "ineffectual," or "inefficient." Only the future, however, and diligent research may reveal documents which will either vindicate, or, at least explain the unfortunate Marine career of Anthony Gale.

Concurrent with the arrest of Commandant Gale on August 30, 1820, Brevet Major Samuel Miller had become "acting" Commandant of the Corps, a post he held until January 2, 1821, at which time the President appointed Brevet Major Archibald Henderson as Lieutenant Colonel of the Marine Corps, with date of commission of October 17, 1820. Thus began what has been so rightfully called "the Henderson Era," an era which was to last through 38 years of growth, tradition, respect and new glory.

A miniature steel engraving of Archibald Henderson, made while he was a young Marine officer.

It is not difficult to imagine the thoughts which filled the mind of Archibald Henderson the first morning he awakened in the Commandant's House. He had inherited a Corps, weakened in morale by circumstances rooted in both the past and present. Its recent Commandant, badgered by the Secretary of the Navy and finally cashiered from the Corps, had left it virtually leaderless for many months. The matter of pay, so dear to the military man's heart, had not improved. A private received between $6 and $10 a month and his chances of drawing even that were doubtful, for it was believed that desertion could be discouraged by withholding a small percentage of his pay until the man's enlistment had expired. Noncommissioned officers' pay started at $8 and climbed to $17, the pay of a sergeant major. Daily rations were 15 to 20 cents and the annual clothing allowance was $30.

A second lieutenant was paid $25 with slight increases for time in the service. Higher officers were salaried accordingly, up to the Commandant's pay which was $75 a month, with $12 monthly allowance for forage and $10 for cord wood to heat his home.

But, if Henderson had inherited an indifferent Corps, he had also inherited a Corps he *wanted,* a Corps he envisioned as the finest fighting military organization in the world—and its home at Eighth & Eye Streets in the Nation's Capital would be a garrison worthy of its elite troops. But, if Archibald Henderson was a man of vision, he was, at once, a man of practical determination. He knew that he could not give his Corps a reputation unless his Corps earned it. And that reputation was necessary to get full cooperation from the Navy Department. His own relations, too, with the Navy would have to be strong and overshadow, by far, those of his predecessor.

His Corps had served its apprenticeship well; now it was time for its leader to turn it into a mature fighting machine. Henderson lost no time in getting started. On an extensive inspection tour he personally took inventory of men, gear and stations. For the most part, he found his men serving with the attitude that nobody cared. But their new Commandant cared. Shrewdly, he knew that pride would have to be bred from within. Time later for the coveted

77

recognition he hoped would come from the Federal Administration.

Henderson's sound reasoning that his Corps would be no better than its officers brought forth one of his first orders: All newly appointed officers would be, for a time, stationed at his own headquarters, Marine Barracks, Washington, where they would receive a vigorous officers' basic training under his personal supervision, before assignment to sea duty. The usual procedure, before the Commandant's order, had been the assignment of junior officers to ships' detachments immediately upon commissioning. At Eighth & Eye he maintained a skeleton battalion, thoroughly indoctrinated in the newest infantry tactics as well as artillery. Further, concise orders were issued to veteran officers at the Corps' posts and stations, intended to discourage indolence if it existed. Officers were ordered to make repeated personal inspections of their commands and, so far as feasible, they would personally hold drills and instruction for their men.

Satisfied with his first step in the direction of a more efficient operation of his Corps, the Commandant turned his attention to administrative matters. More and better uniforms and equipment would give him the standardization he wanted throughout his ill-clad Marine Corps. Toward this end, he made a detailed audit of all appropriated funds and concentrated his efforts on an economic spending program.

Although he ran a taut ship, morale climbed as the men began to realize that their Commandant was personally supervising all matters pertaining to their pay and allowances. Both officers and enlisted were overwhelmed to find Henderson waging an everlasting battle to assure them of their rights in pay, courtesy, proper consideration and rations.

From the beginning, there appears to have been no friction between the new Commandant and the Secretary of Navy, Smith Thompson. Whether the strong-willed 37-year-old Henderson was too much of a match for the 52-year-old Secretary, or whether Thompson's animosity was reserved solely for Anthony Gale has never been recorded but the fact remains that through the terms of 17 additional Secretaries of the Navy, after Thompson's retirement,

Henderson maintained an enduring policy of excellent relations with the Navy. Respect, cordiality and close friendship paid off time and again throughout his command.

Sometime, during his indefatigable first three years as Commandant, Archibald Henderson found time to court a lovely young lady who lived in Alexandria. And, on October 16, 1823, Marine officers and their wives—and Washington society—may have raised their eyebrows when Henderson, a gallant bachelor of 40, whose dinners and supper parties at the Commandant's House had been famous, stepped down to Alexandria and married the 19-year-old Anne Maria Casenove.

Too occupied with the affairs of his Corps to take a wedding trip, Henderson brought his young bride directly to the house where, in celebration, the Commandant had planned a big reception and supper. It was a gala affair, happily upholding the tradition and reputation its host had always enjoyed in the art of entertaining—until after the dinner when the new mistress of the house, leaving the men to their port, strolled into the parlor and found the Commandant's factotum, George, placing a number of small tables about the room at suitable intervals to accommodate chairs.

"What are these tables for, George?" asked the young wife.

"Why, these are the card tables, Mrs. Henderson," the factotum replied, going about his work. "The gentlemen always play cards after supper."

"Well," said the new mistress of the Home of the Commandant, "you may just put them away. No cards will ever be played in my house!"

And, according to family recollections, Anne Maria Henderson's first directive in the house on "G" Street was upheld for the 35 years she lived in the house.

It is doubtful whether the Commandant fought the issue of the cards, or any other issues which might have disturbed his happy family life. Nine children were born to the Hendersons while they occupied the house. Daughters were married in the parlor with Washington notables and high government officials present as well-wishers. Grandchildren were born in the house, and throughout the entire Henderson occupancy, it is apparent that no home in the Nation's Capital could have been more abundant with genuine living.

Henderson's first decade as head of the Corps was sufficiently uneventful to provide the time for the new leader to achieve the efficiency in both the ranks and administration he sought. In 1824, during the Boston Fire, his Marines were called out for rescue work and additional police duties to prevent looting, following the holocaust. Shortly thereafter, one officer and 30 Marines quelled a riot of 238 prisoners in the Massachusetts State Prison when the situation became too desperate for the penal authorities to handle.

These incidents and others like them, although unfortunate, were exactly what Henderson needed to bring his Corps into sharp focus with the American public, for the Commandant had long recognized the political advantages which would follow, if the Marines gained outstanding popularity with the public.

Apparently, through the years, the Commandant's House and the buildings at Marine Barracks, Eighth & Eye, had remained serviceable. On February 20, 1829, however, the Center Building was destroyed by fire. The Commandant immediately reported the disaster in a letter to Secretary of the Navy Samuel T. Southard the next morning.

"The fire," Henderson wrote, "is supposed to have been caused by burning the chimneys in the forenoon, and to have communicated itself to the interior of the third story by some imperfection in them. The two wings were saved by the preserving and arduous exertions of the different fire companies, and the citizens generally . . ."

An appropriation was made by Congress for the rebuilding of the Center House, but evidently it was insufficient since more damage had been done than had been originally estimated. On November 27, 1829, Quartermaster of the Corps, Major Elijah J. Weed, wrote to the Secretary of the Navy, requesting an additional $3,000. Undoubtedly, the request was granted, since the Secretary was being harassed by letters from Marine officers politely demanding reimbursement for rent they were paying to private landlords while awaiting the completion of the Center House.

Action for Marines in the early 1830's was, for the most part, confined to peacetime duty, except for a major incident in Sumatra on February 7, 1832, when Marines from the U. S. frigate *Potomac* landed at Quallah Battoo and burned the village in retaliation for a piratical attack on an American merchant vessel.

By November, 1832, the Barracks buildings, now a quarter of a century old, were in need of repair. In addition, a hospital on the compound had been proposed. In an estimate for "support of the Quartermasters department for the year 1833" a sum of $8,000

Marines and civilians fought the fire which destroyed the original Center House on February 20, 1829.

was requested for "considerable repairs—and there being no Hospital or suitable place for sick at Headquarters . . ."

In the two years which followed, some repairs were made, but the hospital project was delayed until 1834, when bids and contracts for carpentry work and masonry were finally settled. The Barracks, however, continued to deteriorate faster than workmen could repair them. On October 7, 1832, the Commandant wrote to the Secretary of the Navy, requesting authority to replace "the building occupied by the officer on guard . . . and also for the repairs of the stable and the erection of a building to hold the public straw . . ."

Subsequently, Quartermaster Weed submitted a report to the Commandant, emphasizing the housing plight at the Washington Navy Yard, Norfolk, Pensacola and Headquarters. "The Men's Barracks [in Washington] are in bad condition," the report stated. "The North Wing requires a new Roof and all the rooms new floors. The Officers of the Staff have been allowed House Rent. The Public Quarters not being sufficient for their accommodation. . . ."

Official correspondence concerning the Barracks and the Commandant's House dropped off sharply during the following year, but on November 7, 1835, a letter to Henderson from his Quartermaster stated that "the Quarters of the Commandant of the Corps and the walls around the Barracks Yard at Head Quarters are in need of Repair . . ." A sum of $15,000 would be needed for the Washington expenditures and other work to be done at the Marine Barracks at Portsmouth, N.H.

Here, it must be noted that the Commandant's House, by name, is seldom mentioned in the requests for appropriations. It may well be that fear of jealousy in the other services whose leaders did not repose in particular, public-maintained town houses, prompted the Quartermaster to include the house as one of the unidentified buildings of the Barracks when he outlined his requisitions.

Five days after the Quartermaster's request for $15,000, the Secretary of the Navy wrote to the Commandant, asking for a breakdown on the total appropriation. In the Quartermaster's reply, he indicated that $3,500 would be spent "for Porticoes to the House occupied by the Commandant of the Corps and necessary repairs . . ." The "porticoes" turned out to be a veranda which was added to the front, or "G" Street, side of the house. At the same time the entire house was repainted. The cost was $3,000, which was $500 less than the original estimate.

Not too long afterward, a cast iron fence, costing $400, was erected to separate the Commandant's House from the Parade Ground.

In December 1835, a new war began. Indians in Florida massacred an Army column en route from Fort Brooke on Tampa Bay to Fort King. Florida slaves had, for a long while, been making their escapes permanent by joining the Seminole Indians, and in many cases, intermarrying. Southern landowners complained bitterly to the Government and eventually a treaty was made with the Seminoles. Under its terms, the Indians would be taken under Federal protection and assigned to reservations. The Seminoles, however, rebelled when they discovered that the reservations were situated on a plot of ground now occupied by the State of Arizona. It is doubtful whether the reconnaissance party sent out by the Indians actually reached Arizona, but their disparaging remarks upon the party's return may have started the war. "Snow covers the ground," they reported, "and frost chills the bodies of men." A poor recommendation to the bronzed Seminoles who had for centuries lolled in the balmy, resort breezes of Florida.

In the early months of 1836, the Army had borne the combat load, playing a frustrating game of chase with the elusive Indians in the Everglades. Marines from the U.S. frigate *Constellation*, the U. S. sloop *St. Louis* and the sloop *Vandalia* had participated in the fighting. Early in spring, Commandant Henderson wrote a letter to President Andrew Jackson, volunteering a regiment of Marines to support the Army in its war with the Seminoles. On May 21, the President accepted, ordering *all* available Marines to report to the Army.

Henderson, although 53 years of age, chose to lead his men in the jungles of the Everglades in pursuit of the renegade redskins.

Gathering together nearly all of his officers, he reduced shore station detachments to a mere sergeants' guard, and leaving behind only those unfit for duty, he managed to muster almost half the entire strength of his Corps.

On May 24, 1836, Colonel Commandant Henderson reported to the War Department for duty in compliance with the President's order. On June 1, he placed Lieutenant Colonel R. D. Wainwright in charge of Marine Barracks, Eighth & Eye. His letter to the Colonel is a masterpiece of succinct detail.

"Sir," the departing Commandant wrote, "During my absence on the Campaign against the Creek Indians, I leave you in command at Head Quarters. There will be little other than bureau duty to attend to, with which you are so familiar as to render it unnecessary to give you detailed instructions.

"Three Sergts. (for duty) 1 Corpl. & 12 privates are left to furnish a guard for the Navy Yard, to consist of 1 Sergt., 1 Corpl. & 6 privates. One of the music left behind will have to act lance Corporal as a relief for the guard at the Navy Yard. The Sergt Major will sleep in Barracks. Corpl. Brown has always been detailed to attend to the grounds and outside porches around the House occupied by me; I have to request that he be so continued unless it should be necessary to give him other employment or duty.

"Sergt. Triquet is left to assist in attending to the duties at Head Quarters. He is a respectable old man, and has no other failing than that which but too often attends an old soldier; he has however almost corrected this habit.

"I leave you a most valuable Soldier in the Sergt. Major whose health entirely incapacitates him from going on the expedition. He is anxious to go but as a matter of duty I have ordered him to remain, as I cannot take any other than ablebodied men on such arduous Service."

Apparently, Archibald Henderson had intended to go to war with the flourish which was so characteristic of every action he took; he had intended to take the band along! However, the second from last paragraph of his letter indicates that he changed his mind.

84

"Since writing the above," he informed Wainwright, "I have decided to leave the Band, and you will be pleased to divide it into two guards to keep up one Sentinel at Head Quarters. The Drum and Fife Majors, will take alternate days with the Sergt. Major to remain in Barracks in charge of them, so that one of those non-Commissioned officers will be at all times within them.

"My clerk Mr. Fulmer, can take charge of the School in Barracks until the regular teacher returns, and can at the same time, attend to the business of his office."

While Henderson and his force of 38 officers and 424 enlisted were in Florida, Wainwright's initiative accomplished the building and repairs which had been planned before the Commandant's departure.

On July 11, 1836, Wainwright, continuing with the same determination so characteristic of the absent Commandant, complained to the Secretary of the Navy that: "The Barracks at Head Quarters have been for a long time in ruinous State so much so, that the Quarter Master last year Estimated for the erection of New ones: The roof on the South wing being decayed and leaky the rooms are scarcely habitable . . ."

Subsequently, a board of survey, consisting of two captains, a lieutenant, a master mason and a carpenter, were ordered to make a report which would be submitted to the Secretary.

On October 14th, the Acting Surgeon at the newly built hospital, pleaded with Wainwright to furnish surgical instruments and apparatus for the hospital which had been constructed but never furnished. "Complete setts of Trepaning—Amputating, Lithotomy —Eye, Ear, Teeth, etc. instruments with all the necessary apparatus for fractures and dislocations are required and should be procured immediately," the surgeon urged.

The letter concluded with a recommendation that the instruments be purchased in Philadelphia because they were cheaper there.

Wainwright also found himself plagued with a plot of ground he didn't quite know what to do with. It was a small cemetery

A new fence, built in 1837, separated the CMC's House from the parade ground.

which had been reserved for Marines and Sailors. However, since it was not enclosed by a fence, the public had been burying their dead on it. His letter to the Secretary of the Navy on December 14, 1836, speaks for itself.

"Sir," he wrote, "The subject of the burying Grounds for the Marines at Head Quarters has been brought to my notice: To save expense to the public it has been located on a back corner of the Hospital Ground but it is without fence, and entirely exposed to the ravages of Cattle, etc. it is also used as a place of burial by persons . . . who are too poor & worthless to pay in other places.

"A decent respect for the feelings of the Soldiers, and to show that a respectable last home is provided for them, would excite a greatful pride that might be usefull to the recruiting Service.

"Under these circumstances, I have to request Authority to enclose for the use of the Marines the place of interment they have used as such for the last Twenty or Thirty Years."

That Wainwright was awarded his fence, and recruiters of the day could again use the cemetery as an inducement for enlistment is evidenced in a report to Henderson from his quartermaster after the Commandant's return from Florida. The report details eight "New" improvements, seven of which were accomplished in Henderson's absence.

The report was headed: "Statement of Expenditures At Head Quarters M.C. for new objects of improvements Since 1834, according to recollection." The improvements were itemized from memory, since the government accounting department had refused to go through the files to find the actual vouchers.

The impressive list included: "New Hospital and Bathhouse—the former having a two story porch for the benefit of the Convalescent, erected in 1834-35. Cost about . . . $6,000.

"New roof on South Wing of Barracks receiling all the rooms in that Wing—and new flooring & plastering many of them—in 1836-7. $6,000.

"Rebuilding pillars of Arcade which were in a dilapidated state and threatened, in their fall, a portion of the Barracks & relaying new Curb Stone along said pillars for their Support. $800.

"New pavements from the Barracks to the Staff Offices, and around the Barrack front of Centre House, and a new gutter along the whole line of Arcade, 1836-7. $500.

"New fence from the Staff Offices to the Armory and a new fence Seperating the enclosure set apart for the Commdts Quarters from the parade ground. 1837. $400.

"New porch at Commdt's Quarters and painting Said Quarters. 1836-7. $3,000.

"New fence—Around Burying ground—for Marines & Sailors. Six feet high—200 feet long on each side. Well finished and painted in 1837. $500.

"New Vault for safe keeping The QrMaster books. $150."

Early in the summer of 1837, Commandant Henderson had

returned to Washington with his troops. He had lost 61 Marines. A few died as a result of hostile fire; the remainder succumbed to disease. In addition, he had also "lost" two companies, totaling 189 men and officers, who had remained behind. These men were stationed along the Florida coast, around the Keys and with the Mosquito Fleet. With his entire Corps numbering less than a thousand men, the Commandant was still having difficulty fulfilling his commitments—without the loss of two companies serving where he considered their presence unnecessary. He spent the next five years battling to get them back, stating that he no longer had "men sufficient even for an ordinary morning parade, or for a company drill."

For a few years, following Henderson's return from the Seminole War, the Quartermaster at Eighth & Eye was kept busy with requisitions and requests for appropriations to repair the Barracks and to improve and enlarge the Commandant's House. Among the requests was a plea for a fire engine. "There is no engine or apparatus except buckets belonging to the Head Quarters of the Marine Corps . . ." the Quartermaster's letter states. "It is clear that a good engine . . . under the management of an efficient company would be a great protection . . ."

The myriad bills and allowances for painting, building, plastering and masonry seem to have been settled amicably—all but one. Throughout the Commandant's correspondence during 1836 and 1837 one item in use in the Commandant's House seems to have caused a good deal of contention between Archibald Henderson and the Treasury Department.

It all began when the Commandant's Quartermaster bought a Nott stove for use in the Commandant's House before Henderson returned from the Seminole Campaign. A subsequent notice from the "4th Auditor" after Henderson's return informed the Commandant that the stove was apparently a luxury item, and, therefore, not something for which the U.S. Government would pay.

A letter to the Commandant from the 4th Auditor, Treasury Department, dated July 14, 1838, read in part:

"In the settlement of the accounts of the late Quartermaster of Marines . . . the following sums . . .

"For Nott Stove not allowed—see letter . . . this office 28 May & 9 June . . . $98.80.

"To the liquidation of which I have to call your attention, other wise the Pay Master will be instructed to Check the amount from your pay."

On July 17, 1838, the Commandant wrote to the Secretary of the Navy:

"The third Item is for a Nott Stove in the large entry of my Quarters. This was ordered by the Quarter Master as a *fixture*. Without it the house is extremely uncomfortable and it may very properly be considered in the same light with a grate always furnished by the Government."

Almost to the day, a year later, the Commandant was still being harassed by the 4th Auditor. Again he wrote to the Secretary of the Navy:

"An account for a Nott Stove for the passage of the House I occupy has been charged to me by the 4th Auditor. The pipe of this stove passes thro the wall of the house and it appears to me is as much a fixture as a grate. Such stoves have heretofore been allowed to Quarters smaller than mine.

"I forgot to mention this yesterday and request your approval of the account if you think it right to do so."

Evidently approval by the Secretary for payment of the stove was forthcoming, since no further correspondence ensued. Unless, of course, Henderson paid for the stove himself, which is doubtful.

In the 1840's, the house which had remained for 34 years just as the original architect had designed it, except for its new veranda, underwent its first major changes. A two-story annex was added to the northeast corner, enlarging the dining room. It provided an extra window and allowed space for a butler's pantry along the eastern side of the dining room and a back hall and service stairs. On the second floor, the size of the bedroom over the dining room was increased and a bathroom was installed, the

only one in the house until 1914. In this same decade, a one-story addition was built on the west side of the house.

During the following six years, up to the formal declaration of war with Mexico, the Corps' strength hovered around 1,200 men, serving on shore stations and as ships' detachments. At Marine Barracks, Washington, the troops continued to train and perform guard duty, in addition to standing by as a force in readiness if they were needed in the Capital.

In 1842, the Commandant requisitioned artillery for training purposes at Headquarters, New York, Boston, Norfolk, Philadelphia, Portsmouth, and Pensacola. His letter to the Secretary of Navy, A. P. Upshur, read, in part:

"Under a belief that practical instruction in Artillery will render the Marine Corps more useful to the Country, I enclose for your sanction a requisition for two pieces of Artillery for each Station. In case the Corps is increased so as to furnish anything like an adequate protection to the public property in the Navy Yards, practical instruction in Artillery duty can be carried on in conjunction with the other duties of the guard.

**In the early 1840's, artillery efficiency
was increased by training with 18-pounders.**

"Ordnance for the Marine Corps.

"Requiring for instruction and practice of Marines . . . two eighteen-pounders at each post."

During this period, also, $300 was requested by Henderson "for repairs and painting of the Quarters occupied by myself as Commandant of the Corps."

On November 1, 1842, a letter from Henderson, probably sparked by a rumor that the government might provide funds for additional furniture at the Barracks, was delivered to the Secretary:

"Sir," the letter began, "The Centre House occupied by the Subaltern officers of the Corps stationed at Headquarters contains four rooms down stairs and four in the second story. Plain furniture would answer for these quarters.

"The House occupied by the Commandant of the Corps contains four rooms on the first floor and four in the second story. In case the Dept. decides to allow articles of furniture for the last house, the present occupant does not wish any articles except for the four rooms on the first floor. Both the houses have a passage."

Although no record remains to identify the furniture which was "allowed," the correspondence does indicate that Commandant Henderson never passed up an opportunity to keep his Barracks and house provided for. Even an estimate for a new "wood house" which sheltered the logs for the fireplaces was sent to the Secretary for sanction because "The old one is tumbling down and is beyond repairs."

Although six years had passed since Archibald Henderson had led his Marines against the Seminoles in support of the Army, his devotion and leadership had not been forgotten. On March 4, 1843, he was promoted to Brevet Brigadier General for his service in Florida.

By September 1843, the Commandant had apparently noted that the various Navy Yards had begun to develop their own libraries.

In consequence, he addressed the Secretary again in a brief note.

"Sir," he wrote, "A Library at the Head Quarters of the Corps would be eminently beneficial to the officers. I would therefore ask the sanction of the Dept. to the enclosed list of books . . ."

On the reverse of the original letter are two short comments by the "Dept."

"Allow it." And, "ansd. Oct. 2"

The books ranged from Maury's Navigation to Gibbons' Decline and Fall of the Roman Empire to Plutarch's Lives and "An Encyclopedia (Cheap Edition)." Although there are 54 titles on the list, not one of them appears to have been intended for off-duty, pleasure reading.

During the next three years unrest had begun to grow in a vast piece of real estate, called by the Mexicans, "Tejas." Here, in this sparsely settled land, Americans had built homes and formed the Republic of Texas. The "republic" had been admitted to the Union, but a controversy over the designation of the Rio Grande as a boundary rekindled old Mexican contentions for ownership. Battles had already begun to rage when, on May 13, 1846, the United States formally declared war on Mexico.

But, this time, Henderson, now 63 years of age, decided to stay home and direct the destinies of his Corps from its home at Marine Barracks. An order from the Secretary of the Navy on May 21, 1847, directed the formation of a Marine regiment under Lieutenant Colonel Samuel Watson, for duty in support of the Army under the command of Lieutenant General Winfield Scott. Sixty-three men from Marine Barracks, Washington, joined the newly formed regiment at Fort Hamilton, New York, and sailed for Vera Cruz. At Puebla, Mexico, they became a part of General Scott's Army when he began his march on Mexico City. However, he left a small detachment of unhappy Marines to guard the sick and wounded and the supply dump. Again, at St. Augustine, he ordered the Marines, now brigaded with the Second Pennsylvania Volunteers, to remain in reserve.

But, the disconsolate Marines did not remain in reserve for long. When Scott attacked the approaches to the Citadel of Chapultepec, he found Mexican resistance furious and formidable. He called on the Marines. Chapultepec, two and a half miles from the capital, seemed to sneer down on the Americans like a monstrous rock dragon. The fortress was built high on a ridge, walled in on the north, east and south by other ridges which rose to 200 feet above the plain. The only approach was the west road—lined with stone blockhouses. On August 12, 1847, American artillery battered the fortress. After a Marine reconnaissance mission, an attack was planned for the next day.

During the night, two assault parties of more than 500 Marines and Army volunteers were formed to spearhead the attack on the Citadel. A pioneer force of 70 Marines and Soldiers was equipped with scaling ladders, crowbars and pick axes. Two support groups of Marines were led by Lieutenant Colonel Samuel Watson and Major Levi Twiggs.

At dawn, American artillery again bombarded the stronghold. The Mexicans answered, inflicting casualties on the U. S. troops. Under the heavy shelling, the assault force crept up the slope until they were in a position to attack. On a given signal, the American cannon ceased firing, and the Marines attacked.

The battle which followed was a bloody hand-to-hand, close combat melee of savage bayonets, swords and rifle butts. Major Twiggs, a former commanding officer at Marine Barracks, was mortally wounded by gunfire. Later, the Americans poured through a breach and the Citadel fell.

A small Army detachment was left to guard the fallen fortress and the Marines and Soldiers began their advance toward Mexico City. By late afternoon, they encountered strongly manned enemy artillery and deadly fire from Mexican riflemen as they attempted to break through the gates defending the city. By evening, the first gate had been taken and the second fell shortly thereafter.

The night began with furious attacks by the Mexicans, all of them repelled by the Marines and Soldiers. Gradually, Mexican fire became sporadic and at daybreak on September 14, 1847, the Americans glanced skyward and saw the welcome sight of a white flag hanging limply from the National Palace flagpole. Eight

ARCHIBALD HENDERSON
Fifth Commandant

Marines had been killed or died from wounds and 24 others had been wounded. In his report to Washington, General Scott said of the Marines: "I placed them where the hardest work was to be accomplished, and I never once found my confidence in them misplaced . . ."

The victory at Mexico City paved the way for the peace treaty between the United States and Mexico which was concluded on February 2, 1848. Settlement of the southern boundary of Texas gave the nation a state, and the battle for Mexico City gave the Corps the first line in its Marine Hymn, "From the Halls of Montezuma . . ." which was written shortly after the occupation of the city.

From 1844 to the close of the Mexican War, repairs and innovations at the Barracks and Commandant's quarters continued. The Commandant's House was awarded a new double privy—cost $35. The hospital and the Center House each received two coats of paint. In the "best Plain Manner," the hospital estimate for painting was $175, the Center House $270, which included varnish for the doors on the first floor. A bid for a new roof for the carriage house and stable, attached to the Commandant's House, was set at $125.

In November 1844, Henderson noted that the paint on his house was blistering and scaled. A succinct note to John Y. Mason, Secretary of the Navy, followed.

"Sir," Henderson complained, "I enclose to the Dept. surveys and estimates . . . for painting the exterior of the Quarters of the Commandant of the Corps. The Commandant's House has not been painted for many years, and it has now become necessary to paint it to prevent its decay."

On the reverse side of the original letter is a brief note in the Secretary's handwriting: "Let the expenditure be made . . . J.Y.M."

By 1846, the basement floors in the Commandant's House had begun to rot. It was discovered that water seepage was the cause. A well "for the purpose of draining the basement room" was ordered, estimate: $30. With the "sinking" of the well, a dry basement was assured; another $14 was allowed for plastering the walls.

The same year, allowances for a few more repairs were requested. They included: "a new grate in dining room—$25; Setting grate in parlor—$9; new area steps & repair of pavement—$9; new steps for west portico—$10; laying gutter from cistern pump—$3; and painting 3 Porticos & 2 Small Rooms—$70."

1847 marked Archibald Henderson's 27th year of residency in the Commandant's House which was now 41 years old. Along with a survey of urgent repairs for the Barracks, a list of items for the preservation and appearance of the house was included. The survey board found "the repairs specified in the accompanying Estimate indispensably necessary." They were for: "Repairs of lead roof—$14; 2 Circular gutters South Side—$10.80; Painting N.E. room 1st Story & S.E. room 2nd Story—$46.25; Papering N.W. room 1st Story & S.E. room 2nd Story—$36; Painting South Porch—$15; Painting Paling fence in front—$29.25; Repairs of brick work at Stable—$15; Repairs of brick work of South Porch—$5; and Putting paling fence in front—$35."

The decade following the close of the Mexican War was an interlude of uneasy peace for Henderson's Corps which had grown high in stature, but remained low in number. On October 31, 1850, its strength was 70 officers and 1,210 enlisted. While about half the Corps was engaged in training and shore duty, Marines serving as ships' detachments were going ashore to protect American lives and property in the Latin American countries. In 1853, Marines played an important role in peaceful missions to persuade Japan to open her trade to the rest of the world. As a diplomatic gesture, a naval expedition under Commodore Matthew Perry, with a Marine detachment of six officers and 200 enlisted men, sailed for Okinawa and Japan where their display of military pageantry so captivated the Japanese that it opened the way for The Treaty of Peace, Commerce and Navigation which was signed on March 31, 1854, making Japan one of the greatest trading nations in the world.

However, while diplomatic relations were being developed with Japan, trouble had begun to grow in China with Britain and France. American lives and interests had become endangered and, by the fall of 1856, U. S. ships were in Chinese waters, landing Marines to protect American property. At Canton, 181 Marines and Sailors went ashore where they manned fortifications around the American compound. On their return to their ships in gunboats, a Chinese fort opened fire on the men. In answer to the unprovoked act, U.S. ships began a series of attacks on Chinese forts until, on November 16, 1856, an emissary of the Imperial Commissioner of Canton came aboard the American flagship and offered regrets for the original attack on the gunboats. The apology ended the hostilities.

A few blocks from his own doorstep, Commandant Henderson could hear the rumblings of trouble when, in 1857, Washington election issues were being bitterly contested. In a desperate attempt to control the election, the "Know-Nothing" Party had brought in gangs of hired thugs, known as "Plug-Uglies," from Baltimore to threaten physical harm to voters and eventually seize the polling places throughout the Capital to halt the elections.

The bullying had begun early on Monday morning, June 1, 1857, and Civil Authorities, unable to quell the rioting, had asked the President for help. At 10 A.M. Henderson was handed an order directing him to send the whole force from the Marine Barracks to

Marines from the Eighth & Eye garrison dispersed the election rioters in 1857.

prevent bloodshed at the polls. Under an "experienced officer" the troops were to report immediately to the Mayor for "all necessary instructions."

"The force," Commandant Henderson wrote in a report, headed simply, *Statement of Occurrences on Monday, June 1,* "was prepared with all possible dispatch and the cartridge boxes filled with ball cartridges. . . It was formed in line and I addressed a few words to the troops. . ."

Henderson, now 74 years of age, did not attempt to lead them, but placed Captain Henry B. Tyler in command. The Marines moved out from Eighth & Eye Streets about noon on their march to City Hall, but their Commandant preferred the theater of operations to his rocking chair. In civilian clothes, he also headed for City Hall. He arrived there just as the Marines were deploying in front of the building.

"I repaired to the office of the Mayor," Henderson's report stated, "and offered my services to him, as a citizen to aid him in the performance of his duty. He accepted my offer very cordially. . ."

The Commandant followed the Mayor out into the street where he heard rumors that a cannon had been set up near the market. Satisfying himself, by further inquiries, that the rumors were true, Henderson told the Mayor to have Captain Tyler order one of the two companies to capture it. The question immediately arises: Why did the Commandant make the Mayor responsible for giving the order? The simple answer is in his report: He wanted to beat the Marines to the cannon.

"I preceded this detail," the report states, "with an intention of ascertaining the exact position of the gun, as well as the intention of those around it. I passed near it, saw that it was pointed down the street, but was then not in a position to bear on the approaching line of Marines. I then decided to place myself in such a position as to prevent its being so pointed as to do harm to the advancing line. I passed quickly to the rear of the gun and advanced towards its muzzle and placed myself between the gun & the street along which the troops were advancing, with my knee against the gun near its mouth and kept it there, until the right of the advancing line had passed it. The line was then halted, faced to the front at shoulder arms. No order having been given to capture the gun and finding those who manned it, preparing to fire it, I stepped rapidly over the street and said to Capt. Tyler, 'now is the time to order the capture.' He gave the order and I said to Major Zeilin, 'the soldiers quick, quick,' and with a rapid charge the rioters were driven from the gun.

"By the capture of the gun my fullest desire was affected. It ceased to be a rallying point for the rioters and deprived them of all chance of taking the lives either of the troops or the citizens. . ."

After the capture of the cannon, the Plug-Uglies continued to fire pistols and revolvers which were answered by the Marines until the rioters appeared to have given up the fight. Henderson, convinced that the street skirmish had ended, ordered the Marines to hold their fire. Evidently, a few of them didn't get the word.

"I requested those near me to cease firing and put my umbrella under the gun of a tall Sergt., believing that the rout was complete," the Commandant wrote, "but I had scarcely done so when a man came rapidly through one of the openings in the Market House, discharging a pistol in the direction of the Sergt. & myself and turned to save himself by flight. A gun was fired at him by the Sergt. . . . and I jumped forward and seized him by the collar and made him prisoner. I . . . took him to the Mayor and told him I had seen the man discharge his pistol directly where we were standing . . . I returned to the gun which had been hauled over to the east side of the street . . . I found it was, to all appearances, heavily charged. . ."

The capture of the cannon and the presence of the Marines from the Eighth & Eye compound undoubtedly ended the riots, for Commandant Henderson, after delivering his prisoner to the Mayor, was requested to report to the President. There, he provided an account of the action.

The year, 1858, was uneventful for the Corps. A few ships' detachments went ashore in Uruguay and Paraguay to protect American lives and property, and 20 Marines from the Washington Barracks were called out to restore order at the city jail. The Corps' strength was at a new high of 63 officers and 1,789 enlisted men and its reputation as a dependable force in readiness had reached an unprecedented stature.

It was on this excellent plane of efficiency that Archibald Henderson left his beloved Corps, when on January 6, 1859, he returned from a brisk walk, lay down on a sofa before supper, and died quietly in his sleep.

Funeral services for Colonel Commandant Henderson were conducted at the Marine Barracks on January 10th. President Buchanan, his cabinet and many high ranking officers of the other services attended. The President is said to have walked behind the hearse from the Barracks to the old Congressional Cemetery in Southeast Washington where the Commandant was interred.

Archibald Henderson was survived by his wife, Anne Maria, who followed him in death 13 days after he had passed away, and by three daughters and three sons. One son, Charles A. Henderson, had been commissioned a second lieutenant in the Corps and had fought in the Mexican War. During his father's declining years he had acted as the Commandant's aide.

It was inevitable that the decades to come would produce their own legendary characters, but of them all, none surpassed the legends which grew and surrounded the memory of Archibald Henderson. One of these concerns his will. The tale has been passed, down through the years, that Henderson, having been the master of the house on "G" Street for more than 38 years, had forgotten that it belonged to the government, and had tried to will it to his wife. The legend, of course, is not true, since the will which settled the Henderson estate, made on May 1, 1847, contains only one reference to the house—and that delineates only personal property. In part, it reads:

"I do hereby give and devise to my wife Anne Maria Henderson all my real and personal estate . . ." A full description followed, including: "All the furniture in the house now occupied by my family, except such as belongs to the United States, a list of which is in the hands of the Quarter Master—also two carriages and four horses and all other articles about the house—two female slaves Betty and Dinah, one very old. . ."

Although the tale about the will is easily disproved, there are other Henderson legends which are more difficult to explain. It has been said that the spirit of the Commandant who lived for so many years in the house occasionally returns to pay his respects—in one way or another.

There is a story that the wife of a much later Commandant awoke during her first night in the house and found an elderly man with a white fringed beard and wearing a historic Marine dress uniform, sitting quietly in a chair before the smoldering embers of her bedroom fireplace. Whether the lady screamed or remained frozen with fear has not been recorded, but the man, aware that his presence was being observed, arose, bowed politely, then vanished. The following morning, she described her visitor of the previous night. When the Commandant returned home that evening, he brought with him a portrait of General Henderson.

"That," said his wife, looking intently at the painting, "is the gray-bearded gentleman who was in my room last night!"

Many years later, on February 13, 1943, another Commandant, General Thomas Holcomb, was entertaining dinner guests in the house. He happened to mention that, among other affairs that day, he had signed an order, establishing the Women's Reserve.

"Old Archibald," he said, "would turn over in his grave if he ever found out that females could become commissioned officers in his beloved Marine Corps!"

The words had scarcely been spoken when Henderson's portrait, which hung over the sideboard, came crashing to the floor.

If, indeed, these legends of Archibald Henderson's metaphysical visitations are true, it may also be true that he reserves his manifestations for the old house, knowing that his spirit with which the young Marine Corps was so thoroughly imbued, still remains strong in the Marine of today who needs no reminder from the past to help him uphold the glory of his Corps.

The tenure of Archibald Henderson had left the Corps solidly established, well prepared and highly respected, but his death had left the Corps in need of a new leader who would follow in Henderson's dynamic steps. Unfortunately, seniority ruled out the selection of any officer whose young vitality might have prevented a decline and given the Corps a brilliant record in the field, as well as in naval engagements in the Rebellion between the States which hovered on the horizon. The senior officer at the time of Henderson's death was John Harris, a lieutenant colonel in his late sixties,

JOHN HARRIS
Sixth Commandant

with 45 years of Marine Corps service. To Harris, on January 7, 1859, fell the responsibilities of the Corps when he was promoted to colonel and named Commandant.

Although the new master of the Commandant's House had been a career Marine with wide combat experience, his organizational capabilities and zeal did not match those of his predecessor. However, the affairs of the Corps in the interval of peace prior to the Civil War were handled efficiently.

The tremors from the South, felt in Washington during the early months of 1859, exploded into a serious incident when on the night of October 16th, John Brown, a fanatic abolitionist, captured the Federal Arsenal at Harper's Ferry. Brown, obsessed with the idea of stamping out slavery on an independent level by force, had managed to purchase a farm near Harper's Ferry in the fall of the year, and secretly use it for his headquarters. With about 20 followers, he infiltrated the sleeping village, took the arsenal and captured local citizens for hostages. He then sent out an order for all slaves to flee their masters and join him at Harper's Ferry. Even in the immediate vicinity his call went unheeded.

The State Militias of Virginia and Maryland were sent to put down the insurrection. In addition, the Secretary of the Navy ordered all the available Marines from Marine Barracks, Washington, under Lieutenant Israel Greene, to Harper's Ferry to retake the arsenal. Colonel Robert E. Lee was in command. Both Lee and his aide, Lieutenant J. E. B. Stuart, were Army officers.

The militia sharpshooters had little trouble scaring Brown's men in the village, and by nightfall, his forces had thinned to less than half. With his hostages and remaining supporters, he barricaded himself behind the heavy oak doors of the fire house within the arsenal and determined to make his hopeless stand.

On October 17th, at about 11:00 P.M., Greene arrived with 86 Marines from the Washington Barracks, and the two Army officers. Lee sent Stuart, under a flag of truce, to the engine house to demand Brown's surrender. When Brown refused, Lee decided to wait until daybreak before attempting to capture Brown and set the hostages free.

The next morning at sunrise, Stuart again tried to persuade Brown to surrender. "Never," the abolitionist replied. "I prefer to die here!"

Now, with the professional Marines on the scene, the volunteer militia refused to attack. Lieutenant Greene called his men to attention, saluted Lee and outlined his plan. A storming party of 12 Marines would use only bayonets in the attack, thus preventing injury to the hostages. Three men with sledge hammers would batter down the oak doors. Lee again asked Brown to surrender and was met with the third refusal. At a nod from Lee, the Marines attacked.

But, the sturdy oak timbers of the doors would not yield to the pounding of the sledge hammers. A heavy ladder was brought and used as a battering ram. This time the oak splintered and a huge hole admitted the Marines. Armed only with a light ceremonial sword, Lieutenant Greene was the first man through the breach. Two blasts from Brown's rifle missed Greene, but one round killed a Marine private just behind Greene.

The young lieutenant slashed at Brown, inflicting severe gashes around the neck and shoulders. A final, powerful stroke brought the abolitionist to the ground. With Brown a prisoner, all resistance ended. Under Marine guard, the rebels were taken to Charlestown and tried for treason. Brown recovered from his

wounds, was found guilty and hanged. Eighty-six Marines had left the Washington Barracks; 85 returned.

A month later, on November 18, 1859, Commandant Harris evidently discovered an unpaid bill relating to the John Brown incident.

"Sir," Harris wrote to Isaac Toucey, the Secretary of the Navy, "I enclose to the Department, a memorandum of bills, for provisions furnished the Marines, while at Harper's Ferry — amounting to $67.32½.

**One Marine from the Barracks was killed in
the attack at Harper's Ferry where the
abolitionist, John Brown, was captured.**

"I respectfully request authorization to pay them. . ."
The bill was enclosed with the letter. It read:
"To A. Kelly, for cheese, crackers and ale .... $ 9.70
"To Mr. Richards for bread 8.15
"To Mrs. Butler for hams, coffee, etc. 10.12½
"To Charles Johnson for hams, cheese and crackers 25.35
"To Washington Cox for coffin, etc. 14.00
$67.32½

The year 1860 passed uneventfully for the Corps, with little action, other than the protection of American lives and property in various countries where internal trouble threatened. At Marine Barracks, Washington, training continued and the Marine Band entertained constantly at White House functions. Repairs and renovations at both the barracks and the Commandant's House received Harris' personal scrutiny and were executed with dispatch.

Two "parlors" in the Commandant's quarters were painted and papered, and much of the woodwork was repainted. The carriage house and stable were repaired, and a requisition was made for 200 feet of fire hose.

Apparently the equipment used with the fire engine, purchased in the late 1830's, had worn out and, when the messenger's stable burned, the hose on hand had proved unserviceable. Harris immediately asked the Secretary of the Navy for authorization to spend $300 for new hose. A number of roofs were also replaced. The roof on the Center House and the roofs on the Commandant's tool room, harness room and coal house were all leaking, and since all would have to be redone, Harris pleaded for "uniformity in their outward appearance," apparently a factor which had escaped planners in the past.

Necessary repairs within the barracks, by 1860, had become so numerous that funds were inadequate. However, the need for paint and plastering on the outside walls of the barracks prompted Harris

to write to the Secretary of the Navy and beg a portion of the allowance to get the work done and keep up appearances — at least
from the viewpoint of the pedestrian on the city streets.

"Sir," he wrote, ". . . In relation to the repairs of the Garrison,
although our funds, under the head of repairs will not admit of the
expenditures asked for, I hope you will authorize a portion of it at
this time. . . that we may improve our outward dilapidated appearance. The inside work can wait until Congress passes the
appropriation."

1860 closed with the secession of South Carolina in December.
Mississippi, Florida, Alabama, Georgia and Louisiana followed in
January 1861. On February 4th, a congress of representatives of
all the southern states who had passed ordinances of secession
before that date, met at Montgomery, Alabama, adopted a provisional constitution and elected Jefferson Davis President of the
Confederate States of America. With war inevitable, Lieutenant
General Winfield Scott, the commanding general of the Federal
armies, issued a confidential, standing operating procedure for the
protection of the Nation's Capital. The orders read:

Headquarters of the Army
Washington, February 12, 1861

"The following general instructions are issued for the government of the troops in this city.

"In case of alarm, every man will instantly proceed to his proper
place, the artillery to their stable, those acting as infantry, to the
parade ground. A Corporal and 4 privates, their dragoons, will
report to the quarters of the General-in-Chief, to bear orders.

"On the instant of alarm, either by day or night, a mounted
messenger from Griffin's Battery, will proceed, at full speed, to the
arsenal, to notify Barry's Battery. Brooks company will be the
guard of Magruder's Battery, Allen's Company the guard for
Griffen's Battery, Haskin's Company, the guard of Berry's Battery.

"Should the troops therefore be suddenly called out, Magruder's
Battery will, at once, occupy the square containing the President's
Mansion and 4 of the executive Departments. A gun near each
angle, Ebzey's company to occupy the Treasury Building.

"Griffin's Battery will in a similar manner guard the General-in-Chief office and patent office. Berry's Battery will take the shortest route and proceed to the vicinity of the Capitol and there await further orders. Haskin's Company will join this Battery.

"The Dragoon will be held in readiness to mount, at there stables.

"In case of alarm, outrage or mob violence, at, or near, any of the public buildings or in the stores or squares of this city, Colonel Harris, Chief of the Marine Corps, will please put at rapid march for the Capitol square, and there wait for further order, as many of his Marines as he can spare from other duties.

"Major General Weightman, with his foot soldiers has charged himself with the care of the bridge including those in Georgetown.

By Command of Lt. Gen. Scott"

Commandant Harris may not have noted the misspelled words, but he did observe that the order had come from the Commanding General of the Army, and not from the President. In consequence, he sent a letter to the Secretary of the Navy, calling his attention to the irregularity in the orders.

"Sir," Harris wrote, "I enclose to the Department a copy of general instructions from Lieutenant General Scott. In acknowledging the receipt of it yesterday, I stated that in accordance with, I have given the necessary instructions to the Marines.

"On reflection, it occurs to me that the necessary order from the President, assigning the Marines with the Army, has not been promulgated. I, therefore, send the accompanying copy of the instructions, for such action as the Department may deem proper, —Regarding that I would not do so in the first instance."

A note, unsigned, undated, and undirected, attached to Harris' letter agreed with the Commandant. It stated simply:

"Your second impressions were entirely right. The Marines had not been detached for service with the Army by the President of the United States. It, of course, would be necessary to subject you to Army orders."

The technicality was eventually resolved, but in the meanwhile, intensive training continued at Marine Barracks, Washington. Harris, proud of his troops, requested the Secretary of the Navy to arrange an appointment for a drill and parade for the President. On February 27, 1861, he wrote:

"Sir, the pleasant weather, which we have had for the last few days, has enabled us to bring our men rapidly forward, so that the officers now think they will do credit to the Corps; and, both they and the men are desirous of a salute to the President, in front of the executive mansion, at any time he could spare half an hour . . . .

"If you approve of the proposition, I respectfully request you will propose it to the President, and acquaint me with the result."

With the nation divided and an unofficial war in progress, a new President was inaugurated on March 4, 1861. When Abraham Lincoln took the oath of office, the Marine Band was there to play for the ceremonies, just as it had played for every inauguration since John Adams had been elected President.

A month after Mr. Lincoln had entered the White House to the strains of Hail To The Chief, the Marine Band's salute, the South affirmed its intention to fight for its secession when, on April 8th, the President of the Confederacy, Jefferson Davis, called for 20,000 volunteers for the Southern forces. President Lincoln countered on April 15th with a plea for 75,000 volunteers to serve with the Federal troops.

The President's call had made the War Between the States a reality. In one year, from June 1860 to June 1861, the active strength of the Corps had risen from 1,801 men to 2,386 officers and enlisted. During the same year, most of the Marines were engaged as ships' detachments or at shore installations, many of them under Confederate threat or actual fire.

At Marine Barracks, Washington, the facilities bulged with the influx of new men. On June 25, 1861, Major John G. Reynolds, Commander of Marines at the post, complained to the Commandant because the stables for his horses had been occupied by newly-arrived recruits. Major Reynolds also requested "improvement of the garrison" which included "enlargement or extension of privy, sleeping quarters, washing and bathing tubs, much needed. . ." Estimates were accepted and a Washington contractor took the plumbing bid.

"Sir," the bid stated, "The cost of building two wash houses at 58 feet, and one 20 feet long, similar to those now in barracks, will cost One Hundred Ninety Dollars.

"The cost of building bath house 24 feet x 11 feet x 10 feet will cost, built in a similar manner, One Hundred Ninety Five Dollars.

"The cost of fitting up 25 iron wash basins supplied with water will be Two Hundred Ninety Four and 75/100.

"The cost of fitting up 6 zinc baths, supplied with waste pipes complete, One Hundred Ninety Seven and 50/100.

"It is contemplated to place all pipes, etc. out of reach of frost and make a permanent job."

Another indication of the extent of the crowded facilities is an estimate for the building of "Cap, Musket, Belt and Drum Racks." Bunks, stairs, and flooring were also included, along with mess tables and benches. The specifications and materials were outlined briefly:

"Cap racks for 240 caps, drum racks, and 20 drums, 6 muskets and belt racks to be 8 foot long.

"The material for the above racks to be dressed [planed] white pine, for Barrack rooms. Musket and Belt racks for 50 muskets to be undressed [rough wood] white pine for temporary Barracks. The whole to be built in a substantial manner for the sum of fifty-five dollars.

"Specification for material and building two outhouses or privys, each to be 30 feet long by 6 feet wide open in front to be built of undress material, with dressed rail. Both houses to be completed for One Hundred Forty Nine and 44/100 and to be roofed with cedar shingles.

"Specification for material and building bunks, stairs, musket, belt and cap racks, and floors in room at south end of Barracks:

"Bunks—There is to be 4 bunks, 19 feet, 6 inches long, by 5 feet wide—Two to be 3 tears high and 2 to be 2 tears high to be built of undress material.

"Stairs—To be of undress material—steps to be 4 x 4 step risers 4 x 4 white pine—Carriages 3 x 12 eastern shore joist.

"Racks—There will be musket, cap and belt racks sufficient for 60 men, built of dress material.

"Floors—There will be two floors, 27 feet x 25 feet; 7 Inches wide, First story floor to have sleeps [timbers] of 3 x 4 scantling to be covered with 4/4 thick undressed.

"Second story—The joist to be pearced out to the floor, to be covered with 4/4 undress.

"The whole to be completed for the Sum of One Hundred Forty Seven and 53/100.

"Five tables average length 25½ feet x 2 feet 6 inches wide @ $6.25, $31.25.

Marine Barracks, Washington, D. C., circa 1859-1864, showing the new Center House, left; a portion of the barracks, and the Commandant's House, right.

"Ten Benches average length 25 feet 6 inches x 10 inches wide @ $1.87½, $18.75.

"Sun Screen for protecting temporary mess table over arcade, 100 yards @ 75¢, $75.00."

As the blistering Washington summer approached, Union leaders haggled over the preferred steps to be taken to strangle the baby Confederacy before it could grow to manhood and engulf the Federal government. General Winfield Scott, an old campaigner, recommended the use of Union seapower to smother rebel commerce. However, northern businessmen, for whom the profitable southern markets were temporarily cut off, were impatient and, realizing that Scott's strategy would be time-consuming, demanded a direct thrust at Richmond, the heart of the Confederacy.

Politics and economics triumphed, and Scott was left with his maps and a firm conviction that, although an attack on Richmond might have a fifty-fifty chance, the probability of reaching the city was a hundred to one. To begin, the Federal Army would have to march halfway across Virginia to get there;

its troops were composed, for the most part, of local militiamen
with less than 90 days of training; and along the way, somewhere,
a Southern army lay in wait—an army whose potential was still an
unknown capability.

Emotional fever was high in Washington, along with climbing
July temperatures, when Scott eventually was forced to place
General Irving McDowell in charge of the Federal Army with
orders to take Richmond and put an end to the seditionist nonsense.

The Union forces who marched out of the Nation's Capital included a battalion of Marines from the Eighth & Eye barracks,
commanded by Major John Reynolds. Of his 12 officers and 341
enlisted men, only five officers and nine noncommissioned officers
had had military experience; the rest were raw recruits. Fortunately,
for the major, his troops were placed in support of the "West Point
Battery," a regular Army artillery unit which had been trained at
the Military Academy.

The march on Richmond, more than a hundred miles away,
ended abruptly 26 miles from Washington at Bull Run on July 21st,
when the Federal troops found a strong Confederate army which
forced the Union troops into one of the most ungallant retreats in
American history.

Back in Washington, the Union forces had time to contemplate
their enemy whom they had so grossly underestimated. At Marine
Barracks, Major Reynolds sat, disconsolately, penning a four-page
report to his Commandant on his Marines' role in the encounter.

". . . On reaching the field," the report reads, in part, "and for
some hours previously, the battery's accelerated march was such as
to keep my command, more or less, in double-quick time; consequently the men became fatigued or exhausted in strength. Being
obliged at this period to halt, in order to afford those in the rear
an opportunity of closing up and taking their proper place in the

line, the battery was lost to protection from the force under my command.

"Upon our arrival at the battlefield the position of the battery was pointed out, and I was directed to afford the necessary support. In taking the position the battalion was exposed to a galling fire. While holding it, General McDowell ordered the battalion to cover or support the Fourteenth New York Regiment, which was about to be engaged. The battalion, in consequence, took the position indicated by the general, but was unable to hold it, owing to the heavy fire which was opened upon them. They broke several times, but were as frequently formed and urged back to their position, when finally a general rout took place, in which the Marines participated. . . . The abrupt and hasty retreat from the field of battle presents a deplorable deficiency in both arms and equipment."

Reynolds had placed a share of the blame on arms and equipment. Eight had been killed and the Marines had lost in the battle 18 wounded and 14 missing. An accelerated training program was urgent to turn the new recruits into combat Marines. On July 25, 1861, the training burden became even heavier when Congress authorized an increase in the strength of the Corps to 93 officers and 3,074 enlisted.

With the defeat at Bull Run, the strategy of the Union forces turned to Scott's originally proposed use of seapower, and ships' detachments strained the Corps' numbers, making Marine participation in land campaigns almost impossible.

At Marine Barracks, Commandant Harris was having a difficult time keeping his Marines "at home" for the training they needed. Continually, he complained to the Secretary of the Navy that his men were being used for various chores which he felt could be handled by the Army. A letter to Secretary Gideon Welles on October 15, 1861, stated:

"Sir, the President of the United States was at the Navy Yard last evening, and informed Captain Dahlgren that 60 Army prisoners would be sent down for him to take charge of, and he sent to ask me to aid him in that duty, for that purpose, I dispatched one Sergeant, 1 Corporal, and 30 Privates to the Navy Yard. These frequent calls for men interfere very much with my efforts to prepare for, *the contemplated wishes of the Department,* and I hope the security of these prisoners will be provided for in some other way.

"I also beg leave to recommend that the 40 odd Marines that are stationed at the fort, near Alexandria, may be withdrawn; and, that that duty be performed by the troops stationed near it. Our men require a great deal of drill to make them good soldiers, and this cannot be done while they are constantly on guard, as they are at Alexandria."

It is somewhat surprising that in the midst of a war and the pressing problems it entailed, Commandant Harris managed to achieve legislative status for the Marine Band which, under Lincoln's administration, had continued to gain high popularity, both at the White House and with the Washington public.

In a letter to the Secretary of the Navy, Harris had requested that, by Congressional action, the Band should be accorded the official recognition it deserved. He asked for a statutory strength of one Principal Musician at a monthly salary of $90; seven first-class musicians at $34; eight second-class musicians at $21; and 15 third-class musicians at $17 a month. A Drum Major would be retained, but the old grade of Fife Major would be discontinued.

The request was approved by the Secretary and President Lincoln before it went to Congress. Congress passed the bill, and for the first time, the Band was recognized, separately, by law. On July 25, 1861, President Lincoln approved the act which provided for "One Drum Major; one Principal Musician, thirty musicians for the Band and sixty drummers and sixty fifers." The Principal Musician was also informally accorded the title of "Leader."

Repairs and increased accommodations at the Washington Barracks received prompt attention along with the demands of the time. Stables were converted into permanent barracks and the inadequacies of troublesome facilities such as the plumbing were remedied. In fact, cries of outrage from the neighbors made sewerage mandatory! On November 4, 1861, Harris pleaded with the Secretary of the Navy to make nearly $5,000 available for the necessary easement.

"Sir," Harris wrote, "I have the honor to submit to the Department an estimate . . . for building a sewer from the Barracks Headquarters to the river.

"The sinks used by the men, notwithstanding the utmost care and attention and exhaustion of every remediable means, have been so offensive during the past summer as to be almost unbearable of the citizens residing in the city, and appeals have been made to me, as well as to the corporate authorities of the city for relief.

"The amount of the estimate seems to be large, but when taking into consideration the expense incurred in order to relieve the inhabitants from the nuisance, together with the fact that the scavinger bill alone amounts to nearly ten times the interest on the sum, I think it would be economical on the part of the government to have a sewer built.

"I, therefore, respectfully recommend its construction upon the estimate submitted, to be paid for out of appropriations for repair of Barracks, or should the Department consider this impracticle, I would ask that authority be given to submit an estimate to Congress for the object."

The following "high-priced" estimate was enclosed with Harris' letter.

"The cost of building sewers . . . with lateral branches, pipe connections, traps, excavations, refilling and grating will be as follows:

"2500 feet of main sewer, including
excavations, etc. and refilling at 1.40.............................3,500.00
"Stench traps, fittings, connections, etc.............................195.00
"900 feet 6 inch cast iron pipe for
connections etc. laid at 80¢.............................720.00

4,415.00

Although the activity at Marine Barracks may have reached frantic proportions during the war years, the size of the Corps continued to hover around the 3,000 mark. By 1863, nearly 100 Marine detachments were aboard the ships of the Navy, acquitting themselves brilliantly. In Washington, Headquarters Marine Corps continued to function efficiently, carrying out the administrative details of the Corps. The Marine Band, not only the President's own, had been heartily adopted by the public as well. Its summer concerts on the south grounds of the White House had become so

**An artist's conception of a concert by the
Marine Band on the White House lawn in 1860.**

popular on the entertainment program of the Capital that when Mrs. Lincoln, sorrowing over the death of her son, had the concerts discontinued, the Secretary of the Navy was deluged with outcries from indignant citizens. In his diary, Gideon Welles recorded:

"Spoke to the President regarding weekly performances of the Marine Band. It has been customary for them to play in the public

grounds south of the Mansion once a week in summer, for many years. Last year it was intermitted, because Mrs. Lincoln objected in consequence of the death of her son. There was grumbling and discontent and there will be more this year if the public are denied the privilege for private reasons. The public will not sympathize in sorrows which are obtrusive and assigned as a reason for depriving them of enjoyments to which they have been accustomed, and it is a mistake. The President said Mrs. Lincoln would not consent, certainly not until after the 4th of July. I stated the case pretty frankly, although the subject is delicate, and suggested that the Band could play in Lafayette Square. Seward and Usher, who were present advised that course. The President told me to do what I thought best."

Five days later, the Welles diary carried this notation:

"We had music from the Marine Band today in Lafayette Square. The people are greatly pleased."

That Gideon Welles was not only a staunch patron of the Band, but a severe critic as well, is evidenced in a terse comment in his diary in 1863. "I directed Colonel Harris," he wrote, "a few days since to instruct the Marine Band when performing on public days to give us more martial and national music. This afternoon they began strong. Nicolay [a Presidential aide] soon came to me aggravated; wanted more finished music to cultivate and refine the popular taste—German and Italian, etc. Told him . . . his refined music entertained the few effeminate and refined; it was unsuited to most of our fighting men, inspired no hearty zeal or rugged purpose. In days of peace we could lull into sentimentality, but should shake it off in these days. Martial music and not operatic airs are best adapted to all."

Commandant Harris did not live to see the end of the war which had posed peculiar problems no other Commandant has ever been asked to solve. The War Between the States, at its outset, left Harris with only those officers, most of them old in years, who remained faithful to their northern states. Half of his leaders had been permitted to leave their Corps in deference to their native southern states, leaving him a small, inexperienced staff to be

JACOB ZEILIN
Seventh Commandant

spread thinly throughout his units. Dissension within his officer ranks did little to sustain the Marine tradition so ably established by Archibald Henderson. The death of John Harris on May 12, 1864, left Secretary of the Navy Gideon Welles with the task of naming a new Commandant, and in view of the mistrust and unsatisfactory relationships within the ranks of the Corps' officers during Harris' tenure, Welles sincerely believed that a younger man should head the Marine Corps. However, seniority had been the rule in the selection of the Commandant, and at the time of Harris' death, all the likely candidates were nearly as old as the former Commandant had been.

The Secretary's choice was a 58-year-old major, Jacob Zeilin, not altogether a young man, but certainly not in his late sixties as Harris had been when he was appointed Commandant. Unfortunately, there were many officers who were senior to the major. In clear conscience, Welles solved the problem by ordering the retirement of all Marine officers senior to Jacob Zeilin.

In his diary, Welles wrote: "To supercede them (the officers) will cause much dissatisfaction. Every man who was over-slaughed and all his friends will be offended with me for what will be deemed an insult. But there is a duty to be performed. . ." Gideon Welles performed his duty, and on June 10, 1864, the day after he had retired all officers who had been senior obstacles, he named Zeilin Commandant with the rank of colonel.

Confronted by the difficulties of a waning war, the new Commandant began his tour with renewed efforts to supply the demand for ships' detachments from his small Corps. Apathy, too, had developed among the military of all services; deserters were too numerous to count. By 1865, the Corps had lost nearly 1,000 men by desertion since the war had begun, a large total, compared to 551, including those Marines killed in action, lost at sea, dead from disease and other causes, and wounded in combat.

Throughout the war, Marines had participated in few land campaigns with the Union Army, and when on April 9, 1865, Lee surrendered to Grant, the bulk of the Corps was aboard ships or serving on Naval shore stations. With the end of hostilities, Congress insisted on drastic reductions in both men and appropriations for the Corps, as well as for the other services. In the years which followed, the strength of the Corps steadily decreased, at times dipping to less than 2,000 men, with two-thirds serving at sea.

Life at Marine Barracks, Washington, lapsed back to the normal schedule of training and various guard duties in the vicinity of the Capital. Facilities continued to fall into disrepair and Commandant Zeilin, in his characteristic efficient manner, called attention to the needs of the Barracks in his annual report to the Secretary of the Navy on October 15, 1866. His direct comments were intended to impress a post-war, parsimonious administration.

"The barracks at Washington," he stated, "were erected in 1805, [Zeilin's guess] more than half a century ago, and although at that time, the plan of construction may have been considered suitable for the accommodation of masses of men, to-day it is considered as wholly inadequate in the important points of light, air, and room.

"But, in addition to these original defects in the design of the buildings, they have become, from long and constant use, in such a dilapidated condition as no longer to be habitable without most extensive repairs. At the instance, therefore, of the quartermaster of the corps, I have recently ordered a survey to be held upon them, and the report of the board not only affirms the opinion of their present condition, but recommends a thorough reconstruction, using as much of the old material in the new work as is possible.

"In view of the above, I have directed the quartermaster to have a suitable plan prepared with estimates of cost, to be submitted to the department for approval; and as this work is believed to be really necessary for the future health and comfort of the men, I earnestly ask for it the favorable notice of the department."

In anticipation of approval for new construction at the Barracks, Commandant Zeilin instructed his Quartermaster to hold a survey and accept estimates. By November 21st, Quartermaster W. B. Slack was able to report his findings to the Commandant.

"I have the honor, Sir," Slack stated, "to enclose a report of the board of survey, held upon the Marine Barracks, Washington, D. C. . . .

"In connection with this report, I was directed by the Commandant of the Corps, to procure a suitable plan for the reconstruction of these Barracks, with estimate of the cost of same.

"I have now the honor to submit the estimated cost of putting up the buildings contemplated, amounting to One Hundred Thirty Eight Thousand, Nine Hundred dollars.

"A photographic view of the plan of buildings is also enclosed. This estimate is believed to be reasonable, and in view of the absolute necessity for the work, May I ask for it the favorable consideration of the Department.

> I am, Sir
> Very respectfully
> W. B. Slack, Quartermaster

Approved and forwarded J. Zeilin
Colonel Commandant
To: Honorable Gideon Welles
    Secretary of the Navy

But, prices had gone up. The sum of $138,900 was a lot more than any Commandant had ever requested for a building program at the Barracks, and apparently Colonel Zeilin's plea was either rejected or ignored. One year later, in his annual report on October 14, 1867, he again urged rebuilding of the Barracks, but this time he cut the estimate in half. . . .

1859-1875 Marine Band dress uniforms. Left to right: Sergeant Major, Chief Musician, Drum Major, Musician.

"I would again earnestly call the attention of the department," he wrote, "to the condition of the barracks at this station, and would renew the recommendations made in my last annual report, for their entire reconstruction. A board of officers, accompanied by the civil engineer and two master mechanics of the navy yard, have recently made a thorough re-examination of the quarters, and are of the opinion it would be a useless expenditure of money to attempt their repair.

"The quartermaster of the corps has heretofore again submitted estimates for their reconstruction, of which I would respectfully ask for your approval. And in view of the fact mentioned in his letter, that the sum required for the erection of one wing (which is all that is desired at present) will not increase the expenditures beyond the amount appropriated for the support of his department last year, I sincerely trust that Congress may be induced to grant the sum desired. . ."

Enclosed with the Commandant's annual report was the Quartermaster's summary of estimates. It stated:

"Sixty-nine thousand, four hundred and fifty dollars is asked to rebuild one-half of the Marine Barracks, Washington, D.C.

"These buildings have been condemned by a board of survey, as entirely unsuitable for quartering masses of men, and an estimate of the cost of rebuilding, amounting to $138,900, has been submitted by a competent architect, but as only one-half of the barracks can conveniently be constructed at a time, only half the entire appropriation is asked for at this time. In connection with this estimate the report of the board of survey and the estimate of the architect are submitted."

Another year went by, and still a thrifty administration refused to rebuild. Zeilin, again in his annual report, persisted in his attempt to procure an allocation for the reconstruction of the Barracks. On October 19, 1868, he wrote:

"While fully recognizing the necessity of a curtailment of all public expenditures, I cannot but feel it my duty to renew the recommendations so often made for an appropriation to rebuild the barracks at this station.

"These quarters were erected in the year 1800 [another guess] and are consequently about the oldest structures now in this city, and are doubtless the oldest barracks in the country.

"They were originally very imperfectly built, and of very inferior material; they are now rapidly crumbling to decay, and becoming so dilapidated, that it will be utterly impossible for the troops to occupy them much longer.

"When it is considered that the Headquarters of the Corps is the principal Marine station, the only school of instruction for the officers and recruits entering the service, and that consequently a pretty large force of men should at all times be stationed here, I feel assured Congress would not regard an appropriation to reconstruct these barracks as an unnecessary expenditure, even at the present time, when the utmost economy is demanded.

"I trust, therefore, the department may not deem it inconsistent with its views of retrenchment to recommend the desired appropriation."

Again, the Commandant's pleas went unfulfilled. Undoubtedly, frustrated, discouraged and now convinced that no money would be forthcoming, Zeilin left the chore for his successor.

But if the Commandant failed to stir the administration into a reconstruction program at Marine Barracks, he did succeed in keeping a high degree of efficiency within his Corps. In spite of a drastic reduction of personnel and steadily decreasing allowances, he managed to supply guard detachments for vast quantities of naval supplies and the many ships which were being decommissioned. He made personal annual inspections of neighboring Marine posts and stations, and when the new Army drill and tactics were adopted by the Corps in 1867, Zeilin ordered all Marines both at sea and ashore to be thoroughly indoctrinated in them.

And, while the officers and men at Eighth & Eye Streets fought the battles of leaking roofs, tumbling arcade supports and rusty plumbing, the widespread detachments were quelling riots, protecting lives and property abroad and performing their general peacetime duties as a force in readiness wherever trouble spots developed.

In spite of the worldwide services constantly provided by these detachments, a movement to absorb the Corps within the Navy grew to dangerous proportions. That the Corps remained a separate military organization, functioning under its own headquarters at Eighth & Eye, is due, for the most part, to the strong and direct efforts of Jacob Zeilin. His defense of his Corps in a situation which might well have annihilated it, might be viewed as a parting gift. He retired shortly thereafter on November 1, 1876.

The new Commandant, Charles G. McCawley, inherited a Corps still suffering under the post-Civil War reactionary attitude of both the public and the government toward the regular military establishments. The strength of his Corps remained around a static 2,000 men and its meager support came from appropriations enacted grudgingly and with indifferent tardiness.

Along with McCawley's program for many improvements within the Marine Corps were the deteriorating barracks at Eighth & Eye. Undaunted by the failure of his predecessor, the Commandant began the battle on a new tack. A fire in a stable gave McCawley an opening and a logical handle on which to hang his recommendations. In a summary to Secretary of the Navy W. C. Whitney, McCawley wrote:

CHARLES G. McCAWLEY
Eighth Commandant

"Sir, I have to report that a fire broke out in the upper part of a wooden building used as a stable, and storehouse for straw, (which is kept for filling bedsacks for the enlisted men) at the Marine Barracks, Washington, D.C.

"Prompt measures were taken to save everything in the building. The Government horse, wagon, harness, etc. were all saved uninjured. Nothing belonging to the Govt was destroyed, but a portion of the frame building which it is not necessary to rebuild. It was originally built of old lumber, and by the Post carpenter. A part remains uninjured which can be repaired as a stable and carriage house for the mail wagon and horse. . . .

"Efficient aid was rendered by the Navy Yard steam fire engine, manned by the Marines from the Barracks there . . ."

Commandant McCawley's hopes for new buildings at the Barracks were to be founded on the threats of destruction by fire which would wipe out all the records of the Corps since its beginning. He emphasized this danger in an annual report to the Secretary.

"The item," he wrote, "in the estimates now submitted of $25,000 for the erection of a fire-proof building for use as offices of commandant, adjutant and inspector, paymaster, and quartermaster at the headquarters of the Corps is necessary, in view of the fact that the buildings now occupied for the purposes named are small frame structures, exposed to danger from fire liable to originate at any moment in frame tenement houses in the immediate vicinity.

"There are no vaults or other means in the offices for the protection of the archives against loss either by fire or burglars; and when it is considered that all the records of the Corps from 1787 to the present time are on file in the offices now occupied, embracing valuable and important papers required as evidence of service of enlisted men, upon which must be based all information relative to claims for pensions, bounties, etc., as well as all vouchers upon which moneys heretofore appropriated by Congress for the support of the Corps have been expended, it will at once be seen that the destruction of the present office buildings, with their contents, by fire would be a calamity; hence, the absolute necessity for the appropriation in question."

Commandant McCawley's request for a $25,000 building fund met with the same defeat which had discouraged Jacob Zeilin. Other items, however, received attention. In a letter to the Secretary, McCawley pointed out the need for furnishings in a room at the Commandant's House where he met with official visitors.

"Sir," McCawley stated, "I respectfully report to you that in my quarters there is a small room used by me as a library and office for the transaction of official business after office hours which has never been furnished by the Government.

"I request that authority be given to purchase for it the following articles, viz:

1 Lounge or Sofa
2 Arm Chairs
4 Chairs
1 Desk
1 carpet and
1 rug, at such prices as may be deemed proper by the Department."

But, the office furnishings were a small expenditure, compared to the $7,550 Congress appropriated for the renovation of the Commandant's House in the same year it had rejected his request to rebuild a portion of the Barracks. Although the work on the house was not completed until after McCawley had retired, it included allowances for the repairs and changes his board of survey had recommended. The old attic was converted into a third floor, the roof was rebuilt and a second story was added over the west wing. The veranda, on "G" Street, erected while Archibald Henderson was Commandant, was removed and the front acquired a "town house" appearance.

At the barracks, the Commandant's band was seldom at home. During McCawley's tenure its popularity had risen to celebrity proportions. Favored and acclaimed by press and public alike, it played at inaugurals, concerts, weddings and other special national and social affairs. McCawley, well aware that the band had firmly established itself in the Capital, included a request for additional Congressional recognition of the band when he penned his annual report to the Secretary of the Navy.

"I renew my recommendation of last year," he wrote, "that the *band* of the Marine Corps, being properly a national band (as it is used for all official purposes in Washington, and sometimes elsewhere), should in justice to the worthy men who have, many of them, served faithfully for long periods, be put upon a proper footing by Congress as regards classes and pay . . ."

Although there seemed to be no greater heights for the band to climb, it had been Commandant McCawley's choice of a new leader back in 1880 that had given the band its golden age. It would seem almost coincidentally appropriate that McCawley's appointment had named a man who had spent many hours of his childhood playing on the lawn in the garden of the Commandant's House and watching the band march on the drill field in preparation for its parades. The band's new leader, John Philip Sousa, was the son of Antonio Sousa, a Portuguese musician who played in the Marine Band. Also a skilled carpenter, the elder Sousa, in his off-duty hours, performed minor repairs on the Commandant's House.

When young John Philip reached the age of 13, wanderlust took over and his father expressed deep concern about the boy to then

127

Commandant Jacob Zeilin. Believing that the discipline and training, traditionally a Marine characteristic, would develop character in
the youth, he asked Zeilin to enlist his son as an apprentice music.
The Commandant agreed, and John Philip began a seven-year enlistment in the Corps. Well prepared with a musical education
under his father's tutelage which had begun at the age of six,

Sousa applied himself diligently to the task of becoming a bandsman. He also received military training and was taught to "read, write and cipher as far as the single rule of three." To defray the expense of his scholastic sessions, one dollar was deducted from his pay each month.

After his first tour of duty, Sousa reenlisted and he and his father were regular members of the Marine Band until 1875, when both received special discharges. The elder Sousa remained in Washington and continued to work for the Commandant as a cabinetmaker. Young John made his way easily in the musical world, and five years later, in 1880, when Commandant McCawley needed a leader for the Marine Band, Sousa was directing a theatre orchestra playing for an opera company. Evidently the Commandant had been able to offer the 26-year-old Conductor terms attractive enough to entice him away from the glamour of the theatrical scene, for, on October 1, 1880, John Philip Sousa took over the baton of the band.

The band gained popularity at open air concerts on the White House grounds and in front of the Capitol, and at state dinners and receptions, where its new conductor introduced many of his original compositions which, in years to come, earned for him the title of "March King." Along with his famous *Stars and Stripes Forever, The Washington Post March,* and others, he composed *Semper Fidelis,* later adopted as the official march of the Corps.

Above left, the Marine Band in 1894. Left, John Philip Sousa, "The March King," was the Band's Leader from 1880 until 1892.

129

Colonel McCawley retired on January 29, 1891, after piloting his Corps through 15 years of post-war doldrums. Despite the apathy of the administration which ignored military needs of the time, he was able to accomplish a few improvements within the Corps. In 1882, he managed to have all new Marine officers appointed from graduates of the Naval Academy, thus raising the standards of the Corps' leaders. Under McCawley, training in both artillery and infantry tactics was updated. Although Commandant McCawley had shown determination in many vigorous attempts to secure necessary legislation for the betterment of the Corps, throughout his career he had met with little more than limited success.

Commandants Harris, Zeilin and McCawley had struggled against heavy odds to keep their Corps highly trained, and efficient in administration, so it was fortunate that the combination of changing times and the right Commandant could elevate the Corps and gain for it the Congressional recognition and action so necessary to provide the funds needed for expansion of facilities, along with an increase in personnel. The appointment of 52-year-old Charles Heywood to Colonel Commandant on June 30, 1891, was an

CHARLES HEYWOOD
Ninth Commandant

School of Application, Marine Barracks, Class of 1894.

excellent choice. Under his leadership in the 12 years to follow, the growth and stature of the Corps were destined to equal, in proportion, the tremendous advance it had made under Archibald Henderson in the first half of the century.

Heywood lost no time in inventorying the needs of his Corps, including the deplorable state of decay into which Marine Barracks, Washington, had fallen. Among other activities at the garrison, the new School of Application, a course of intense training for officers, was taxing facilities and living quarters. The outline of instruction covered infantry tactics, small arms instruction, gunnery, torpedoes, high explosives, electricity, field service and modern tactics, and field entrenchments.

Regarding the urgent reconstruction of the Barracks, Heywood picked up his cue from his predecessor when he warned against the possibility of damage by fire in his annual report to the Secretary of the Navy:

"I desire to present, for the consideration of the Department, the fact that the records of the Marine Corps, both of my office and those of the staff, are stored in two buildings, one of brick and the other and larger one of wood, which are liable at any time to be destroyed by fire, originating in them or in buildings outside the enclosure here, which would in a few minutes obliterate our records since 1798 and thereby cause great loss to the Government.

"I deem it my duty to inform the Department of this fact, and request that some provision be made for the erection of a fireproof building here which would be large enough for the accommodation of the Commandant and staff, with their clerks, and all the records. It is thought such a building could be erected for about $25,000."

Again the administration smiled sympathetically, but denied the request. Undaunted, Commandant Heywood would, in the years to come, repeat his plea many times until, in 1901, a benevolent Congress would untie its purse strings and appropriate $50,000 for a fireproof building. In the meantime, however, the Corps' Commandant was, indeed, a very busy man.

Among his other chores, Heywood found time to design a Good Conduct Medal and have it authorized for Marines. His efforts on behalf of the Marine Band brought renewed recognition from Congress when it enacted legislation to double the number of musicians and place them on a more definite military basis. The Act stated:

"That the band of the United States Marine Corps consist of one leader, with the pay and allowances of a first lieutenant; one second leader, whose pay shall be seventy-five dollars per month, and who shall have the allowances of a sergeant major; thirty first class musicians, whose pay shall be sixty dollars per month; and thirty second class musicians whose pay shall be fifty dollars per month and the allowances of a sergeant; such musicians of the band to have no increased pay for length of service."

The Marine Band, photographed at the Barracks in 1898. William H. Santelman was the leader.

Under Sousa, the band had begun to make its annual concert tours. Requests from civilian managers who handled the tours went through official channels and ended with the Commandant's approval or disapproval. The facets covered were interesting, as evidenced in the Commandant's letter of approval to a New York manager.

"Your letter of the 4th instant," Heywood wrote, "to the Secretary of the Navy, requesting that permission be granted for the Marine Band to make a tour of cities in various parts of the country from March 11 to April 14, was referred to this office for recommendation and duly returned by the under-signed to the Secretary of the Navy with an indorsement recommending that the authority requested be granted. The papers have just been returned to this office with the Department's permission for the band to make the tour in question, starting March 18, to be absent for a period not exceeding six weeks, with the express understanding, however, that before giving a concert in any place, the assent of the musical union there (if any) shall be obtained.

"In accordance with this authority, I will grant six weeks' leave of absence to the leader and the members of the Band to enable them to make the tour."

The first seven years of Heywood's tenure as Commandant were spent in a determined effort, little by little, piece by piece, to increase the size of the Marine Corps and establish more posts and stations throughout the United States and, in Heywood's words, our "colonial possessions." With the sinking of the *Maine* on February 15, 1898, and war with Spain imminent, the Corps was ready with nearly 4,000 men—twice the size of the roster it had held for more than 30 years.

In April, three officers and 164 men from Marine Barracks, Washington, left the Capital for New York City where they became part of the 1st Marine Expeditionary Battalion, composed of 24 officers and 623 enlisted men who sailed on April 22 for Cuba where they took Guantanamo Bay and occupied it until fall. In September, the troops from the Barracks returned to Washington, marched through a downpour of rain and were reviewed by President William McKinley.

Upon their arrival at the Barracks, these veterans of the Spanish American War found three surprising innovations at their garrison. A letter from the Quartermaster to the Commandant proudly described these new features. . . .

"A telegraph instrument was introduced into this office . . . and has proved most convenient and useful in the transaction of official business connected with the procurement, shipment, etc., of stores and supplies.

"There has also been installed at these headquarters a telephone which has been found very convenient and useful in sending and receiving official messages.

"Electric lights have also been introduced at these headquarters, being necessary to enable the officers and clerks here to attend to business at night."

The introduction of electric lights may have slightly reduced the possibility of fire at the Barracks, and the handy telephone would certainly expedite calling in an alarm, but Heywood continued with his pleas for reconstruction. A few new problems, aside from the fire hazard, had developed. These were pointed out in his 1898 report. The inspector of buildings in the District of Columbia had been called in for his opinion. He was just a trifle more succinct than the last four Commandants had been. After enumerating a number of technical defects, his report stated:

"In conclusion, it cannot be expressed in too strong language the dangerous condition of this building; first, from faulty construction; second, from overloading of floor or roof; third, from fire; fourth, and most important, from collapse.

"As to collapse," the report continued, "in case of storm or sudden vibration, the building is likely to immediately collapse, and is therefore dangerous to life and limb."

Again the Commandant asked for $30,000.

In 1899, he wrote a similar letter. This time he requested $35,000.

By 1900, his report to the Secretary had become an echo of a request which had rumbled through several decades. This time he asked for $50,000—and got it!

Along with the fifty thousand, Heywood's request for $4,500 to build a band room with second-story accommodations for 50 troops was also granted.

In the same year, Heywood ordered his Adjutant and Inspector to provide him with a detailed report on the conditions throughout the various facilities of the garrison. The Adjutant's comments bore the overtones of a welfare worker.

Under separate headings, he voiced his indignation:

"Guard Rooms and Cells:

"The cells are old and badly ventilated. . . . The three center cells . . . are said to be infested with bed-bugs.

"Kitchen:

"The sink is too small for the present requirements of the command, and . . . the drain pipe from the sink is too small to properly carry off the water, and becomes clogged up. . . .

"Dormitories:

"The Apprentices' School Room is utilized as sleeping quarters

135

for the enlisted men. It is badly ventilated and hardly fit for the purposes of a dormitory. Thirty-four men are quartered in tents in the lower part of the parade ground, and the men so quartered express entire satisfaction with their accommodations.

"The commanding officer states that the present facilities for lighting the barracks by gas are inadequate, and that the quality of the gas is also poor; but authority has been granted and arrangements are being made to remedy this defect by the supplying of electric lighting facilities.

"Wash Room:

"The accommodations of the wash room, which is simply a shed in rear of the left wing, enlisted men's quarters, without means of heating, are insufficient, there being but twelve bowls or basins for the entire command. . . .

"Bath Room:

"The bathing facilities are not sufficient for the present strength of the command. There are but three tubs and these all require re-painting and enamelling.

"Water Closets:

"The automatic flushing apparatus in two of the closets failed, while under observation. . . .

"Post Bakery:

"The oven in the bakery is in bad condition, both the crown and the bottom being practically burned out. The flooring of the bakeshop is badly worn and requires repairs. The kneading trough leaks, and the walls of the bakery need pointing up and whitewashing.

The Headquarters Detachment on the parade ground at the Center House in about 1888.

"Quarters for Sick:

"Although there is a Surgeon's office and a dispensary, there are no quarters for the sick in barracks outside of the dormitories, all serious cases being immediately sent to the Naval Hospital nearby.

"Library and Barber's Shop:

"For lack of accommodation, the library and barber shop are in the same room. There are about fifty volumes which require rebinding.

"The barber is an enlisted man and is paid a per diem amounting to $15.00 per month out of the amusement fund for his services. The price for shaving is five cents and that of hair cutting ten cents, and a ticket for twenty shaves is issued for $1.00. This arrangement shows a considerable source of revenue for the amusement fund.

"Storeroom for Arms, Accoutrements, etc.:

"Many of the bayonet scabbards recently received show evidences of having been filed or sand-papered. These arms are stated to have been received from on board ship. . . .

"Enlisted Men's Quarters:

"Ceilings and walls of several of the rooms need pointing up and re-kalsomining or re-painting, also a number of panes of glass need replacing.

"The railing of veranda at south end of the barracks requires repairs.

"The attic over enlisted men's quarters, south end of barracks, used for storage purposes, has but one narrow doorway leading to it, and in case of fire it would be almost impossible to save the property stored therein."

As a result of the adjutant's report, many minor repairs were made. A hand-powered elevator to the attic store room over the enlisted men's quarters expedited handling of supplies. Low water pressure in Southeast Washington had made it impossible to force a sufficient supply of water up to the second story of the Commandant's House. To alleviate this condition a large storage tank, with a pump, powered by an electric motor, was installed.

By October 1, 1901, the building intended as a band hall and enlisted quarters, for which $4,500 had been appropriated, was completed, and plans and specifications for a new headquarters office building had been prepared. However, the continued deluge of recruits and additional personnel flowing into the Barracks, brought a decision to move the headquarters of the Corps into the downtown area of Washington. Offices in the Bond building at the corner of New York Avenue and 14th Street were rented. The growth of the Corps under Commandant Heywood had increased administrative chores, demanded far more office space than the Eighth & Eye garrison could provide, and finally deprived the Barracks of the headquarters function it had held for exactly a hundred years. The new fireproof building was built, however, it became probably the most luxurious quarters for enlisted men of its day.

But, Commandant Heywood had only begun. Encouraged by the appropriations he had received, he plunged into a complete reconstruction program for the Barracks. Typical of the driving force he had shown throughout his tenure as Commandant, Heywood made a final audacious request from the Secretary of the Navy. In his annual report in September 1903, he asked for $150,000 to rebuild practically the whole garrison.

"The section of the new building," he stated, "occupied by the enlisted men, is not nearly large enough for the use of the command, and as the old barracks have been condemned by a board of survey as not being fit for further occupancy as quarters for the men, I have directed the quartermaster of the corps to include in his estimates the sum of $150,000 for the purpose of enlarging the present new quarters and providing for a suitable band room, mess hall, and kitchen. If these changes are made, it is proposed to remove the old quarters, take down the wall on Eighth Street, and place a neat iron fence in its stead, which would add greatly to the appearance of the post."

Smedley Butler, center, posed with a group of second lieutenants at the Barracks in 1898. The lieutenant beside Butler wore the sash of the Officer of the Day.

Unfortunately, Commandant Heywood's mandatory retirement at the age of 64 came in the following month on October 2, 1903, less than a year before Congress appropriated the $150,000 for the extensive construction he had advocated.

There is little doubt that Charles Heywood, in his 12-year tour as Commandant, had brought his Corps to a new peak of respect as a force in readiness, expertly trained in the most advanced techniques of infantry and artillery warfare of the era. By constant, well-founded demands, he had increased the strength of the Corps from 2,000 men to nearly 8,000 and raised the number of posts and stations in the States and in our possessions from 11 to 29. At the older posts, antiquated facilities were torn down and the troops enjoyed far better living conditions than in the past. The new stations were built according to Heywood's standards—and whatever increased appropriations he could persuade the Secretary of the Navy to approve.

Among other notable innovations in the Corps, under Heywood, regular rigid examinations for officers were required, and officers' schools were established, assuring the Corps of continued, up-dated proficiency in its leaders. Aware that the infantryman's value in combat depended heavily on his skill with a rifle, Heywood set up a system of target practice and established competition for the Hilton trophy in the National Matches.

Realizing that many enlisted men showed promise of having officer capabilities, he succeeded in getting the enactment of a bill which provided for the appointment of noncommissioned officers to commissioned rank. Along with this opportunity, enlisted men found the rank of gunnery sergeant established permanently, and their enlistments reduced to four years.

Following the retirement of Charles Heywood, Colonel George F. Elliott was promoted to brigadier general and appointed Commandant. Under Elliott, the Corps gained a new champion whose successful dealings with Congress were, in part, the result of personal appearances; when the Commandant spoke at committee meetings, his recommendations were accepted with few modifications. Fiery in temperament, sometimes hot-tempered, but always just and courageous, Elliott, on occasion, did not hesitate to appeal directly to President Theodore Roosevelt, making bold demands

GEORGE FRANK ELLIOTT
Tenth Commandant

when he considered his Corps in need of more men or appropriations.

During the closing months of 1903, and most of the following year, activity in repair and construction at Marine Barracks proceeded at an accelerated pace. Walls and ceilings were replastered and repainted; the electric lighting system was completely rewired and plumbing facilities were either repaired or replaced; stoves, used for heating the officers' and men's quarters, were refitted and in perfect operating condition. The Commandant's House, now nearly a hundred years old, was given a "thorough overhauling."

By September 1904, plans were being drawn for the "construction and completion of an addition . . . including the erection and furnishing of a band room, mess hall, men's kitchen, and gymnasium. . . ." Contracts made within the following year brought the total cost for these new buildings to $155,653.

The years 1906 and 1907 were ones of demolition and reconstruction, converting the garrison to essentially its present appearance. The recently built band hall, with second-story quarters for troops, had become inadequate for the newly enlarged band. Under the new construction, a band concert hall was built, designed with a stage and band "shell," typical of the era. More appropriations, raising the sum for building contracts to $300,000, allowed for the construction of a new barracks block, officers' quarters and a brick wall to replace the crumbling wall of stone. The last of the tottering and condemned buildings to fall under the sledge hammers of workmen was the old Center House. Only the Home of the Commandant remained, its original walls and foundation a perpetual cornerstone of Marine Barracks, Washington, D.C., founded in 1801.

Having lost its headquarters function to an office building in the District of Columbia, the Barracks turned its full attention to training recruits and officers, and ceremonial details. The Marine Band, with its mission, "To provide music when directed by the President of the United States, the Congress of the United States, and the Commandant of the Marine Corps," retained its popularity, continuing to serve at the White House as "The Presi-

Appropriations in the first decade of the Twentieth Century made it possible to redesign and rebuild Marine Barracks, Washington, D. C. The 1905 photo, above, shows the new barracks, completed that year.

Right, laying the first brick of Officers' Row in 1907. Below, the House of the Commandant survived.

At left, construction on the band hall shows a portion of the round "shell." Below, a "topping out" ceremony.

dent's Own" and playing its regular concerts, both outdoors and in its home band hall at Eighth & Eye Streets.

But the Barracks was soon to lose another major function. In 1911, a new, huge recruit depot was established at Parris Island, and the Washington garrison, no longer a boot camp, became the center of the Capital's elite show troops. Then, as in recent years, visitors and dignitaries poured through its gates to marvel at the precision of the Barracks drill teams and to enjoy the inspiring music of the Marine Band.

Commandant Elliott had retired on November 10, 1910, after a distinguished career both as a Marine officer and as a leader of his Corps. His successor, William P. Biddle, served until February 24, 1914, during which time little change took place either within the Corps or at the Eighth & Eye Barracks. Following Biddle's retirement, George Barnett was appointed Commandant for a four-year term, the first Commandant of the Corps to be named for a specific term, according to legislation passed in 1913. Barnett was also the first Commandant who had received his early military training at the U.S. Naval Academy. His tenure as Commandant, including his second term, covered one of the most eventful periods in the history of the Corps. In addition to World War I, expeditions to the Caribbean demanded the services of Marines when serious trouble arose in Haiti and Santo Domingo. The First World War

WILLIAM P. BIDDLE
Eleventh Commandant

GEORGE BARNETT
Twelfth Commandant

greatly expanded the responsibility of the Corps, and, under Barnett, its strength was increased to 3,000 officers and approximately 75,000 enlisted men.

The close of World War I brought with it the task of demobilization and reorganization in which Commandant Barnett proved himself a shrewd and capable administrative leader.

When, on June 30, 1920, John A. Lejeune succeeded Barnett as Major General Commandant, the problem of rebuilding the Corps on a professional military basis was imminent. An intensive recruiting program built the Corps up to a peacetime strength of 20,000 regular enlisted men, and the officer ranks attained nearly double the Corps' prewar number.

JOHN ARCHER LEJEUNE
Thirteenth Commandant

Above, following a tradition, begun in the 1860's, the Marine Band serenaded Commandant Lejeune on New Year's Day, 1927. Below, after more than a century and a half, the Band still claims the title of "The President's Own."

Although the Marine Barracks had lost two of its major functions when Headquarters Marine Corps moved to a downtown office building, and its recruits moved south to Parris Island, it gained a new activity in November 1920, when the Marine Corps Institute brought its books, pencils and postage scales to the garrison.

The Institute, patterned after the International Correspondence Schools, was founded originally to provide Marines with courses of instruction by mail, with the emphasis on vocational training. Along with the Marine Band, the Institute found a home at Eighth & Eye Streets.

Some of the MCI courses may have gone to Marines who continued to occupy Haiti and Santo Domingo for a considerable time after World War I. In 1924, however, the Marines were withdrawn from Santo Domingo but turbulence in China and Nicaragua in 1927 required the services of reinforced brigades for the protection of American interests there. These two expeditions occupied the principal interests of the Corps during the remainder of Lejeune's Commandancy.

Wendell Cushing Neville succeeded Lejeune on March 5, 1929. The expeditionary forces, sent out under Lejeune's direction, remained at their posts and the Corps continued in its traditional role of watchdog in troubled countries throughout the world.

WENDELL CUSHING NEVILLE
Fourteenth Commandant

Neville's Commandancy embraced the early period of the tragic American depression. His Corps began to suffer cutbacks as a result, and dire national circumstances precluded any major changes. Substantial appropriations, however, had been provided by Congress for the permanent development of Quantico as an advanced training base for officers. Notable, in these trying times, was the expansion of the use of Marine aviation with expeditionary forces on the foreign stations. In spite of the depression clouds, the Corps maintained its strength of about 18,000 men.

After the death of Wendell Neville, Major General Ben Hebard Fuller became the Corps' 15th Commandant on July 9, 1930. Now, with the depression weighing heavily on the Federal government, curtailments in Corps appropriations brought sharp reductions in pay and personnel. The recall of expeditionary forces from the Caribbean area, however, made possible the development of the early Fleet Marine Force.

Ben Fuller was transferred to the retired list on March 1, 1934, and John H. Russell was appointed Major General Commandant. Under Russell, education and training in the Corps continued to make substantial progress, and the Fleet Marine Force became the Corps' main activity. The following year, the amphibious doctrine of the Corps was outlined in a formal text, titled, "Tentative

BEN HEBARD FULLER
Fifteenth Commandant

JOHN HENRY RUSSELL, JR.
Sixteenth Commandant

Landing Operations Manual." The guide, written at Marine Corps Schools, was published in 1935. Now, with a Standing Operating Procedure, the Fleet Marine Force went to sea to test and improve its doctrine in exercises with ships of the Navy.

Armament, too, gained importance, and along with the growing Fleet Marine Force, additional military equipment was acquired, giving the FMF a firm foundation for the role it was to play in the impending World War II.

General Russell retired at the statutory age of 64 on November 30, 1936. The new tenant of the Commandant's House was Thomas Holcomb, on whose shoulders would fall the task of build-

THOMAS HOLCOMB
Seventeenth Commandant

ing a Corps whose strength, both in men and arms, would be formidable enough to engage the Japanese as an assault force in the amphibious campaigns across the island-infested Pacific.

In 1936, Holcomb had a Fleet Marine Force of two "brigades" (1500 men), each brigade armed with "two-pounders" as anti-tank weapons—and no artillery heavier than 75 millimeters. Both outfits had small engineer companies, but no medical companies nor shore parties. There were only 158 pilots and 140 planes. And, there were no defense battalions to hold our few Pacific bases.

By late 1941, Thomas Holcomb had developed two half-strength amphibious divisions and provided them with the most effective equipment then available. Seven defense battalions had been formed, along with 14 well-trained aviation squadrons. In addition, the Corps, now totaling 66,000, supplied 33,000 men for non-Fleet Marine Force commitments.

The following two years were marked by tremendous expansion as Holcomb built his Corps to 350,000 men, including three amphibious divisions, with a fourth division in training, 95 aviation squadrons, and 15 defense battalions.

At the age of 64, General Holcomb requested retirement, suggesting that younger blood should carry on and complete the task he had so successfully begun. He was retired on December 31, 1943, and Alexander Vandegrift became the new Commandant.

Vandegrift continued with the same drive which had characterized his predecessor, and met the demands of the last two war years with an additional 125,000 Marines.

At his home garrison, depleted ceremonial troops were overwhelmed with burial details, parades and Capital functions. The Marine Band strained under its tight schedule, programming its music at bond rallies to coincide with the times. Although most of the Corps was occupied with combat operations, Marine Corps Institute enrollments totaled 71,225. In the funeral procession for President Franklin Delano Roosevelt, a battalion of Marines, some from Eighth & Eye, formed a part of the cortege. Two escorts and a color guard accompanied the body to Hyde Park, N.Y.

ALEXANDER ARCHER VANDEGRIFT
Eighteenth Commandant

But, beyond the Marine Barracks compound, half a world away, in the Pacific, the war had come to an end, and the Commandant of the Marine Corps was confronted with the huge administrative task of demobilization—the discharge of thousands of "civilian" Marines who had fought valiantly until war's end, and would now return to private life and their former jobs and professions. Along with demobilization came the problem of re-establishing the Corps on a peacetime basis to meet the needs of the Nation.

With demobilization well under way, and the status of the Corps well preserved, General Vandegrift retired from active service on December 31, 1947. The following day, Clifton B. Cates became the Corps' 19th Commandant.

CLIFTON BLEDSOE CATES
Nineteenth Commandant

Cates began his administration under the pressure of post-war readjustment while the Corps was still being scaled down to peacetime proportions. In 1948, his troops numbered less than 84,000. Cutbacks continued until the outbreak of the Korean Conflict, when the Corps found itself reduced to 75,000 officers and men. However, the Commandant gathered his forces from wherever they could be spared and had the 1st Provisional Marine Brigade on its way to the Far East nine days after his order for its activation.

The urgent need for a full-strength, reinforced Marine division with organic air support meant the mobilization of the entire Organized Reserve. Cates obtained Congressional authorization to call in the Reserve, and 138 units from 126 cities responded. As a result, the First Marine Division (Reinforced) and the First Marine Aircraft Wing were available for the assault on Inchon on September 15, 1950.

General Cates, like so many of his predecessors, continued to urge legislative measures in behalf of his Corps. The passage of Public Law 416 by the 80th Congress, which set the ready combat strength of the Corps at three divisions and three corresponding aircraft wings, is due, in part to his efforts.

Clifton Cates was succeeded by Lemuel C. Shepherd, who became Commandant on January 1, 1952. General Shepherd's

LEMUEL CORNICK SHEPHERD, JR.
Twentieth Commandant

RANDOLPH McCALL PATE
Twenty-first Commandant

tenure was characterized throughout his commandancy by a high degree of personal leadership. One of his first steps was the reorganization of Marine Corps Headquarters along general staff lines. The innovation more clearly defined the areas of responsibility, streamlined administrative procedures, and made possible considerable reductions in personnel.

The passage of Public Law 416 placed the responsibility for establishing the Corps on its new, enlarged foundation directly on General Shepherd's shoulders. The smoothly functioning force in readiness today is evidence of the skill and tact with which he handled his difficult chore. Relations and procedures of the Marine Corps within the Department of the Navy were strengthened and, as the first Marine ever to meet officially with the Joint Chiefs of Staff, he established the Corps' position on a solid footing.

Lemuel Shepherd completed his tour as Commandant on December 31, 1955. Randolph McCall Pate succeeded him on January 1, 1956, and became the 21st Commandant of the Corps. Under Pate, the Corps began to feel the impact of the cold war. In the decade to follow, during the tenures of Commandants Randolph McCall Pate, David M. Shoup and Wallace M. Greene, Jr., the force in readiness built and preserved by its 23 leaders with determination and, sometimes in the face of great odds, would be called on many times to serve its Nation in the Corps' traditional mission.

DAVID MONROE SHOUP
Twenty-second Commandant

As a show of force, Marines landed in Lebanon when rebels threatened to take over the government. Off the shore of Cuba, elements of the 5th Marine Expeditionary Brigade were a manifestation of U.S. warnings to Castro if he did not remove Russian missiles from their sites high in the hills. The missiles were removed and the troops sailed back to San Diego and Del Mar, Calif.

When the cold war again threatened to strike in the Dominican Republic, Marines landed to maintain security until a plan could be evolved, insuring the freedom of the Dominican people to select their own form of government. The 1965 landing in the Dominican Republic wasn't the first for Marines; they had been there before in 1800, 1903, 1904, and in 1916.

WALLACE MARTIN GREENE, JR.
Twenty-third Commandant

General Wallace M. Greene, Jr., the 23rd Commandant, had the task of committing his Marines to combat in Vietnam in a war which became unpopular, both politically and with various segments of the American public. But, as in every other conflict, full-scale or trifling, in which Marines have fought, the war in Vietnam was a war for freedom, and Commandant Greene, undaunted by the conflicting attitudes on the home front, commanded his Corps, confident in the belief that patriotism and everlasting Marine tradition would help to bring the war in Vietnam to a successful consummation.

General Greene's tour as Commandant ended on December 31, 1967, but not before a management revolution had begun in the Corps. Under his future successor, then Lieutenant General Leonard F. Chapman, Jr., HQMC Chief of Staff, a small analysis group had been formed to analyze all management matters. General officers were required to learn automatic data processing and other modern management techniques. Quotas to post-graduate management courses were raised and a team from HQMC toured all major commands to discuss new and improved management systems. The establishment of an Integrated Information System moved ahead with significant strides.

LEONARD F. CHAPMAN, JR.
Twenty-fourth Commandant

Leonard F. Chapman, Jr., became Commandant on January 1, 1968. General Greene had left him in command of 300,000 Marines, still fighting in the most controversial war in American history. With more than a quarter of his Corps in Vietnam under combat commitments, General Chapman took the reins, firm in the belief that the problems of transfer and replacement of personnel and the materiel they needed to fight effectively could be solved by the "programming of people and things."

Although concentration on management may have highlighted the General's tour as Commandant, he never failed to recognize the fact that it took skill, sweat and blood to combat the Viet Cong in Vietnam. To this end, training, discipline, and leadership were his main concerns. Maintaining quality within his Corps also became a top priority and with its numbers being trimmed by the thousands, he adopted a "lean and mean" approach. Professionalism was the key word as he insisted on a hard line of the highest standards in discipline, conduct and military bearing. Although his course may have run at cross currents to much of the rest of the military—and the American society as well—it gained majority support from the Marines most directly affected by his policies.

General Chapman's tenure as Commandant came to a close on December 31, 1971. General Robert E. Cushman, Jr., took over the helm on New Year's Day, 1972. With Marine participation in the Vietnam war drawing to a close, the new Commandant foresaw a transition from combat to the Corps' traditional role as an amphibious Force in Readiness. The number of NATO bi-lateral and combined Regular-Reserve amphibious training exercises was dramatically increased. Sea capability, too, made a significant stride with the launching of the USS *Tarawa,* the first of five multi-purpose, amphibious assault ships, designated LHA's (Landing Helicopter Assault). The *Tarawa,* christened on December 1, 1973, by Mrs. Cushman, gave the Navy its largest and fastest amphibious ship, combining the other capabilities of the older LPH's, LSD's, LKA's and LPD's.

General Cushman, a firm believer in the old Marine saying, "Marines take care of their own," established a strong, meaningful

ROBERT E. CUSHMAN, JR.
Twenty-fifth Commandant

Human Relations Program which demanded quality leadership. Enlisted educational opportunities continued to climb, improving to a point where *any* Marine with a desire and ability to advance himself could do so—from a High School GED equivalency all the way up to a bachelor's degree. Rounding out the Marines-take-care-of-their-own programs were successful efforts to improve the Enlisted Personnel Management System.

Headquarters Marine Corps underwent reorganization in the first comprehensive change since the 1950's. The change functionally realigned Headquarters Marine Corps with the Department of the Navy and Department of Defense organization.

The hard line on standards for regulars and reservists was held, in spite of pressures to relax. The emphasis on quality recruiting was not only sustained but increased, in defiance of the difficulties entailed by the All-Volunteer Force conditions.

During the Easter offensive of 1972, a numerically superior NVA force pushed Republic of Vietnam units out of Quang Tri. Quickly responding to the situation, Marine logistics, air strikes, heli-lifts and standby infantry units offshore contributed greatly to the mobility and morale of allied forces, and Quang Tri was retaken within a week.

Following the cease fire agreement, North Vietnamese troops continued to violate the agreement. Marine Aircraft Groups 15 and

12 assisted the Republic of Vietnam forces in countering the early-April ('72) NVA invasion across the DMZ. The mobility, adaptability and efficiency of Marine units based in Southeast Asia again proved a deterrent to active enemy units.

The traditions of the Corps have been founded and broadened by the Marines who have served in war and peace. But, only the Commandants who have led their elite fighting force can have the full knowledge of the burden of responsibility they carry for their country.

Perhaps a far-reaching example of the patriotism in which each Commandant has placed so much unwavering faith is evident in the thousands of visitors who come to Marine Barracks, Washington, D. C., every Friday evening from May to October to witness the magnificent Evening Parade. Spectators experience an intense feeling of pride and unabashed love of country when, in the course of the parade, the American flag, brightly spotlighted on a darkened field, is lowered to the music of the national anthem.

Two full companies of Marines in Blue-White Dress uniforms, the United States Marine Band, and the Marine Drum and Bugle Corps provide a one-hour performance of brilliant color, split-second precision and unequaled music.

At each parade, the Marine Corps Battle Color, bearing multi-colored streamers representing all battles, campaigns and expeditions in which Marines were engaged, is carried by the Color Guard of the Marine Corps. Custody of the Battle Color is entrusted to Marine Barracks, Washington, in respect for the age, tradition and heritage of the Corps' oldest post.

One of the two companies marching in the Evening Parade, is, surprisingly, a company of "part-time" marchers whose primary duty is the operation of the Marine Corps Institute. It is true, of course, that every Marine in the Corps is expected to march with exceptional precision, but to the spectator, watching the parade, the two companies of crack troops would appear to be specialists in the art of drill. The MCI company are specialists, but their parades are a secondary duty; they are actually specialists in the courses they prepare at the Institute, located at the Washington Navy Yard.

Originally, the Institute's mission was centered on providing instruction by mail on various skills throughout the Corps which would increase the usefulness of Marines in a broad field of vocational capacities. Gradually, the instruction was expanded to include high school subjects and technical and junior college level courses. In 1953, however, stronger emphasis was placed on the professional development of Marines through individual courses slanted toward particular Military Occupational Specialties.

In 1961, MCI enrolled its millionth student. Wherever a Marine may be stationed, in the States or anywhere in the world, he is eligible to choose from any of the 114 courses carried on the MCI list. That Marines are taking advantage of the opportunity offered by the Institute is evidenced by the fact that more than 25,000 pieces of mail go out in one week—and the incoming mail is almost as staggering as students send in lessons, letters and returned courses. There is no charge to the Marine student; MCI sends the materials and even the postage is paid. Upon completion of a course, a certificate is awarded and an entry is made in the student's Service Record Book—a definite asset during promotion periods.

The second company whose precision marching in the Evening Parade draws applause from spectators, is Guard Company, whose home is a barracks at the Washington Navy Yard a short distance from Eighth & Eye Streets. Included in Guard Company is the Silent Drill Team. These troops are featured in the parade in a drill, performed without commands or any other signals for movement.

But, the work load at Eighth & Eye falls to Headquarters and Service Company. Aside from their routine duties of post maintenance, armory chores, and food service, this unit provides the Commandant with his stewards, gardeners and drivers. They are also responsible for around-the-clock security for the Barracks. Although they are a busy outfit, they are often required to fall out honor guards and participate in ceremonial details.

Included in Headquarters and Service Company is the Marine Corps Drum and Bugle Corps. If total hours were tallied, this modern-day version of the old Barracks drums and fifes would be committed approximately six solid months of the year.

**The
Evening
Parade**

Undoubtedly, the most renowned and longest tenant at the Barracks is the Band. Through the years, visiting kings, queens, and other prominent heads of state have been serenaded by its music. Its muffled drums escort war dead to their final resting places, and its fanfares herald the dedication of buildings and ships.

Congressional action, from time to time, during the past century and a half, has raised the status and roster of the Band until it has reached the total of 135 men, along with its director, two assistant directors and a drum major.

Numerous commitments make it impossible to assemble the entire Band for any single performance. However, on a special occasion, a 100-piece marching band may be detailed for an appearance. The Band's versatility makes its vulnerable to numerous demands and it is not unusual for every bandsman on the roster to be engaged at the same moment, playing in either a concert orchestra, a tour band, marching band, string ensemble or a dance orchestra.

Although it is doubtful whether Commandant William Ward Burrows, in 1800, planned a permanent installation for his Corps that would endure through more than a century and a half, it seems nearly an act of providence that the elite Band, the elite troops and the Home of the Marine Commandants should be so firmly rooted at the Corps' oldest landmark on a tiny patch of hallowed land in the Nation's Capital.

THE COMMANDANTS . . .

SAMUEL NICHOLAS

FIRST COMMANDANT
November 28, 1775 to August, 1783

b. 1744, Philadelphia, Pa.;
d. August 27, 1790, Philadelphia, Pa.

SAMUEL NICHOLAS was the first officer commissioned in the Marine Corps by the Second Continental Congress on November 28, 1775, when the President of Congress signed an order making him a captain at the salary of $26⅔ a month.

Nicholas immediately began to enlist Marines in Philadelphia for duty aboard the *Alfred* (formerly the *Black Prince*). The *Alfred* and several other vessels were outfitted and received Marine detachments; then, in the spring of 1776, they sailed to the Bahamas and, at New Providence, they surprised the British garrison.

Captain Nicholas and a landing force of 200 Marines and 50 bluejackets captured the town and the forts which defended it, taking away with them valuable stores and ammunition. This was the first amphibious operation the Marine Corps had ever attempted. Following this successful action, the fleet returned north.

On June 25, 1776, in Philadelphia, Nicholas was promoted to Major of Marines and ordered to "discipline four companies of Marines for guards on frigates . . ." In December of the same year, Major Nicholas received orders to march with three companies of his Marines "to be under the command of his excellency, The Commander in Chief, in operations against the British in New Jersey."

163

The battles of Trenton and Princeton followed. Nicholas and his Marines remained with General Washington's army until the end of winter.

In the spring of 1777, Nicholas returned to Philadelphia and served as Commanding Officer of Marines. His duties, since he exercised general supervision over the Continental Marines, closely coincided with those of the Commandant today.

Throughout the remainder of the war he continued to serve in this capacity in the vicinity of Philadelphia. When the Revolutionary War ended, the Marines, along with the Navy, were temporarily disbanded and, in 1783, Nicholas returned to civilian life. He remained in Philadelphia until his death in 1790.

WILLIAM WARD BURROWS

SECOND COMMANDANT
July 12, 1798, to March 6, 1804

b. Charleston, S. C., January 16, 1758;
d. Washington, D. C., 1805

WILLIAM WARD BURROWS studied law, first in Charleston, S. C., then in London, England. He returned to the Colonies in 1775. He is believed to have fought as a militiaman during the Revolution, although there is no record of his service. After the Revolution, he practiced law in Philadelphia until July 12, 1798, when President John Adams commissioned him Major Commandant of the new Marine Corps, established by an Act of Congress on July 11.

Commandant Burrows' first task was to organize ships' detachments for U. S. vessels being sent into combat against the Navy of France's new First Consul, Napoleon Bonaparte. The Corps' headquarters remained in Philadelphia long enough for him to outfit the ships, establish a training program for his men and organize the Marine Band.

Then, in March of 1800, a small detachment of Marines was sent to Washington, D. C., the new capital of the United States, for guard duty at the Navy Yard. On May 1, 1800, Burrows was promoted to Lieutenant Colonel Commandant and on July 15th, he and his staff left for Washington and set up a temporary headquarters for the Corps in a private house in Georgetown.

In September of 1800, the quasi war with France ended, and Congress called for a reduction in the size of the newly created Naval Forces. Despite the reduction in his troops, the Commandant was successful in maintaining the efficiency and readiness that has long since become a Marine Corps tradition.

The following year more than half of his Marines were serving aboard U. S. vessels, many of which were in the Mediterranean, involved in the Tripolitan War.

During his tenure as Commandant, Burrows established the Marine Barracks, Washington, D. C. This compound, in the middle of the southeast portion of the District, is the Corps' oldest post. Here, too, the Marine Band grew to national prominence. Along with appropriations for the garrison, Burrows also obtained funds with which the Home of the Commandants was built. Although he did not remain the Corps' leader long enough to live in the house, it has been occupied successively by Marine Commandants since it was completed in 1806.

Ill health forced Burrows to resign from the Corps on March 6, 1804. He died just one year after his resignation and was buried in the Presbyterian Cemetery in Georgetown. His remains were removed in 1892 to their present resting place in Arlington National Cemetery.

FRANKLIN WHARTON

THIRD COMMANDANT
March 7, 1804, to September 1, 1818

b. Philadelphia, Pa., July 23, 1767;
d. New York, N. Y., September 1, 1818

F RANKLIN WHARTON, whose prominent and wealthy family had

played an important part in the development of the American Colonies, was commissioned a captain of Marines on August 3, 1798. His first duty station was MB, Philadelphia; however, after several weeks he was assigned to the frigate *United States,* where he served as officer in charge of the vessel's Marine Detachment until the close of the undeclared sea war with France in 1801.

He returned to Philadelphia as CO of Marines there and, on March 6, 1804, he received word of his promotion to the office of Commandant of the Marine Corps.

This was a gigantic undertaking for an officer having only five years' experience as a member of the Corps. However, what he may have lacked in military experience was offset by his vitality, diplomacy and complete faith in his officers and men.

The Marine Corps at that time was engaged in America's war with the Barbary States. Commandant Wharton retained the policies established by his predecessor; he stressed military discipline and neatness; he also prescribed distinctive uniforms for his officers and men.

Within the continental limits of the United States, Marines were needed in Louisiana where a large force of Spanish troops had been massed at its southwestern boundary. Marines of that era were stationed at New Orleans, which had been designated to become the seat of the "monarchy" proposed by Aaron Burr. Volunteer companies, Marines, and other troops patrolled the streets, ready to suppress any attempt at insurrection.

Commandant Wharton also ordered a detachment of Marines to Georgia and Florida in 1811 to cooperate with U. S. Army troops in an attempt to subdue an Indian uprising. Under Colonel Wharton, Marines participated in many important engagements during the War of 1812. They saw action at Annapolis, White House, Va., Portsmouth, Craney Is., Bladensburg, and New Orleans, and fought under General Henry Dearborn on the northern frontier.

At sea, Marines participated in important naval battles, serving aboard the warships and privateers on the Great Lakes, the Atlantic, and the Pacific. They fought under Commodore Oliver Perry on Lake Erie and under Commodore Isaac Chauncey on

Lake Ontario. Aboard the frigate *Constitution,* Marines were important factors in that vessel's engagements with the *Frolic, Reindeer,* and *Avon.* Marines serving aboard the frigate *United States* were commended for their efficiency in its fight with the *Macedonian.*

Lieutenant Colonel Commandant Wharton died September 1, 1818, in New York City, and was buried in Old Trinity Church Yard in New York.

ANTHONY GALE

FOURTH COMMANDANT
March 3, 1819, to October 8, 1820

b. Dublin, Ireland, September 17, 1782;
d. Lincoln County, Ky., 1843

FEWER RECORDS survive concerning Anthony Gale than of any other Commandant of the Corps. For six months following the death of Commandant Lieutenant Colonel Franklin Wharton, the Corps was officially without a leader. However, Archibald Henderson was temporarily at the helm. By March of 1819, the Secretary of the Navy had made his decision and the post of Commandant went to Gale.

The few records which remain indicate that Gale was neither effective nor efficient as the head of the Corps. He was finally removed from office and the Corps on October 8, 1820.

Gale's unfortunate relations with the Secretary of the Navy may have heavily influenced his apparent failure as a leader of the Corps. It is known, however, that many of his orders were countermanded by the Secretary, either because of a clash in personalities or due to an outright dislike for Gale.

Unable to bear the Secretary's meddling in the affairs of the Corps under his Commandancy, Gale courageously wrote a letter to the Secretary, outlining in direct terms a definition of authority, as Gale interpreted it in application to the Corps. Having unburdened his mind, Gale became a heavy drinker, and it was on one of his bouts that the Secretary ordered Gale's arrest which led to his court-martial and sentencing on September 18, 1820.

From Washington, Gale went first to Philadelphia where he spent several months in hospitals, then took up residence in Kentucky. Armed with proof that he had been under the strain of temporary mental derangement while Commandant, he spent 15 years attempting to have his court-martial decision reversed. Eventually, in 1835, the government partially cleared him and awarded him a stipend of $15 a month which was later increased to $25 and continued until his death in 1843 in Stanford, Lincoln County, Kentucky.

ARCHIBALD HENDERSON

FIFTH COMMANDANT
October 17, 1820, to January 6, 1859

b. Colchester, Fairfax County, Va., January 21, 1783;
d. Washington, D. C., January 6, 1859

ARCHIBALD HENDERSON was appointed a second lieutenant in the Marine Corps on June 4, 1806; was promoted to first lieutenant March 3, 1807; to captain April 1, 1811; and appointed a major, by brevet on April 19, 1816, to rank from 1814. As a captain he served aboard the U. S. Frigate *Constitution* and participated in the engagements with the *Cyane* and *Levant* on February 20, 1812.

During the years between the second war with Great Britain, and the year he was appointed Commandant, Henderson was on duty at such posts and stations as Boston, Mass., Portsmouth, N. H., HQMC, and New Orleans, La. The years from 1820 to 1835 were marked by neither unusual nor outstanding activities on the part of the Marine Corps other than its part in the suppression of piracy in the West Indies, and the operations in the early 1830's against the pirates of Quallah Battoo. During the war with the Seminole and Creek Indians in Georgia and Florida in 1836-37, in which the Marine Corps took an active part, Commandant Henderson went into the field with his command which included approximately half the Marine Corps.

For his services in checking Indian hostilities, he was advanced to the rank of brevet brigadier general by the Army.

During the Mexican War, which was preceded by much military activity on the part of the Marine Corps in the years 1845-46 on the West Coast, Henderson ably administered the affairs of the Corps.

In the era between the Mexican War and the Civil War, the Marine Corps, under the ever-watchful eye and direction of Commandant Henderson, was by no means an idle organization. In 1852-53, the Marines took part in the famous expeditions of Commodore Perry to Japan. In 1855, they participated in an expedition to Uruguay as a result of an insurrection at Montevideo, and in 1856, fought an engagement with the hostile Indians at Seattle in the Washington Territory. Also, during the same year, Marines took part in the capture of the Barrier Fort in China.

For more than 38 years, Henderson guided the destiny of the Corps, battling for its position as a strong armed force in the American military structure and, at the same time, attending religiously to every minute administrative detail. When he died in office at age of 76, he left his beloved Marine Corps with an *esprit de corps* and a heritage of tradition.

Archibald Henderson passed away quietly in his sleep in the Home of the Commandants on the afternoon of January 6, 1859. His funeral, conducted at Marine Barracks, Washington, was attended by the President of the United States and the Cabinet along with other high-ranking notables. His remains were interred in the old Congressional Cemetery in Southeast Washington.

JOHN HARRIS

SIXTH COMMANDANT
January 7, 1859, to May 2, 1864

b. East Whiteland, Chester County, Pa., May 20, 1790
d. Washington, D. C., May 12, 1864

JOHN HARRIS entered the Corps as a second lieutenant on April 14, 1814, but there are no records to indicate that he rendered any outstanding services during the War of 1812.

In the years following that war, he was assigned as commander of Marine guards on a number of the larger naval vessels and at various times was stationed at Erie, Philadelphia, Norfolk, New York, and Boston. He rendered conspicuous service with General Archibald Henderson in the Florida Indian wars in 1836-37, in command of a mounted detachment of Marines. For this service he was later awarded the brevet rank of major.

He returned to Washington in March 1837, as the bearer of a treaty which had been made by the Commanding General with the Seminole chiefs. From that time until the Mexican War, he was assigned to routine post duties and recruiting.

During the Mexican War his services were limited. He did not go to the theater of operations until the closing month of the war when he took a battalion of Marines to Mexico, but arrived after the armistice had been concluded. He was sent with his battalion to Alvarado, Mexico, as part of an occupying force, pending negotiations to determine whether or not the Isthmus of Tehuantepec would be placed under American control.

The project failed shortly thereafter and Harris returned to the States and resumed his round of peacetime duties, spending the remainder of the time, until he was made Commandant, in command of the MB at Philadelphia and New York. He was promoted to lieutenant colonel on December 10, 1855, and appointed to the office of Colonel Commandant of the Corps on January 7, 1859— the day following the death of General Archibald Henderson.

Although Harris had succeeded a vigorous, aggressive Commandant, he conducted the peacetime affairs of the Corps satisfactorily until the approach of the Civil War. After the election of Abraham Lincoln as President, the Marine Corps, together with the other military services of the U.S., began to disintegrate when a large proportion of the commissioned personnel resigned to offer their services to their native southern states.

With the actual outbreak of the war, Harris saw his obligations clearly. His position grew more difficult as nearly half of the officers of the Corps resigned, many of them younger officers with particularly distinguished records. Official records fail to disclose any recommendations by Harris for the expansion of the Marine Corps to sufficiently meet the great national emergency. He seemed to have been content with supplying Marines to guard shore establishments of the navy and supplying Marine detachments for the larger vessels.

The record of the Marine Corps in the Civil War and during the remainder of Harris' tour as Commandant was brilliantly successful concerning men serving on naval vessels, but negligible when fighting on shore.

Harris' tour as Commandant and his long career of 50 years as a Marine officer came to its close when he died in Washington on May 12, 1864.

JACOB ZEILIN

SEVENTH COMMANDANT
June 10, 1864, to October 31, 1876

b. Philadelphia, Pa., July 16, 1806;
d. Washington, D. C., November 18, 1880

JACOB ZEILIN was appointed a second lieutenant in the Marine Corps on October 1, 1831. After completing training at Marine Barracks in Washington, D. C., his first tours of duty were ashore at the MB Philadelphia, and at Gosport (Portsmouth), Va. He then served aboard the sloop of war *Erie* in March 1832, after which followed a tour of duty at Charlestown (Boston), Mass. In August 1834, he again joined the sloop *Erie* on a long and eventful voyage that lasted for more than three years.

He was promoted to first lieutenant September 12, 1836. From September 1837 to April 1841, Zeilin served at Charlestown, Mass. and New York. In February 1842, he returned to sea duty on board the *Columbus;* during the cruise that followed he spent several months on the Brazil station. Upon the conclusion of this tour of sea duty, and after again serving at important Stateside Marine Corps stations on the East Coast from 1842 to 1845, he was transferred to duty aboard the frigate *Congress.*

During the conquest of California (1846-1847), he took part in the capture and occupation of Santa Barbara and San Pedro early in August 1846, and thereafter assisted in the first capture of Los Angeles. A few days later, with the Marines of the squadron, he recaptured San Pedro, which had been lost to the insurgent Californians.

In December 1846, when General Kearney's army was beleaguered at San Bernardo Ranch, Calif., Zeilin took a prominent part in its relief and rescue. In January 1847, he served as adjutant of Commodore Stockton's mixed column of Sailors, Marines, and volunteers who marched from San Diego and defeated the Californians in the battle of San Gabriel and in the affair at La Mesa.

On January 28, 1847, he was appointed Military Commandant of San Diego and served in that capacity until the completion of the conquest of California.

Zeilin was promoted to the regular rank of captain on September 14, 1847. During the following few months, together with the Marines of the Pacific Squadron, he participated in the capture of important ports in Lower California and the west coast of Mexico, and served as Fleet Marine Officer of the Pacific Squadron.

After the close of the war with Mexico, Zeilin proceeded to Norfolk, Va., where he served for a time, then went to New York.

He remained in New York until June 1852, when he was selected to accompany Commodore Perry as Fleet Marine Officer in the famous expedition to Japan in which the Marines played a prominent part. Zeilin himself was the second person to set foot on shore at the formal landing of the naval forces at Yokohama on July 14, 1853. He was also one of those later accorded special honor for his part in the expedition that opened the doors of the Mikado's realm to the outside world.

Upon his return from Japan, he was again stationed at Norfolk. This duty was followed by command at the MB, Navy Yard, Washington, D. C. After remaining for a time at Washington, he again went to sea, this time aboard the frigate *Wabash* on the European Station. He remained on this assignment until the year 1859. During the early part of the Civil War, he was on garrison duty in command of Marine Barracks, first at Philadelphia and later at Washington, D. C. In July 1861, he was on detached duty with the Marine battalion at the Battle of Bull Run as a company commander and was wounded in that action. Five days later he was appointed to the regular rank of major.

In 1863, Major Zeilin was given command of the battalion of Marines sent to support the naval force whose mission was the capture of Charleston, S. C. But, because of illness, he returned after a few weeks to garrison duty at Marine Barracks, Portsmouth, N. H.

While serving at Portsmouth, he was appointed Colonel Commandant of the Marine Corps on June 10, 1864. His faithful and efficient performance of the duties of Commandant of the Corps during the trying period of the last year of the Civil War and those years immediately following it, is evidenced by the fact that he was promoted to the rank of brigadier general on March 2, 1867. Brigadier General Jacob Zeilin retired on November 1, 1876, after having served more than 45 years as a Marine Corps officer.

His death occurred in Washington, D. C., on November 18, 1880.

CHARLES G. MC CAWLEY

EIGHTH COMMANDANT
November 1, 1876, to January 29, 1891

b. Philadelphia, Pa., January 29, 1827;
d. Rosemont, Pa., October 13, 1891

CHARLES MC CAWLEY was appointed a second lieutenant in the Marine Corps on March 3, 1847, and served during the war with Mexico. He participated in the storming of the Castle of Chapultepec and taking of the City of Mexico, being brevetted first lieutenant for gallant and meritorious conduct in these actions.

He served throughout the Civil War and, in May 1862, he was ordered with a detachment of Marines to reoccupy the Norfolk Navy Yard and aid in the destruction of large stores of ammunition which would otherwise have fallen into the hands of the Confederate forces. He also aided in the capture of Port Royal, S.C., and served with a battalion of Marines on Morris Is. during the bombardment and destruction of Fort Sumter and the capture of Forts Wagner and Gregg.

Mc Cawley commanded a detachment of 100 officers and men in the boat attack on Fort Sumter, September 8, 1863, and received a brevet as major for meritorious conduct during this engagement.

In 1876, he was appointed to the highest post in the Marine Corps, Colonel Commandant. One of Colonel Mc Cawley's first duties as Commandant was to dispatch Marines to eastern cities where labor riots had gone beyond control of local state authorities. In each instance, the disorders were quelled shortly after the arrival of the Marines.

Among other accomplishments attributed to his tenure was a plan that resulted in the assignment of several members of each graduating class of the U. S. Naval Academy to the Marine Corps as second lieutenants. The Quartermaster Department, under Commandant Mc Cawley, became more self-sustaining by manufacturing a considerable portion of its own equipment at its supply depot in Philadelphia. In 1880, he assigned John Philip Sousa to serve as leader of the Marine Corps Band.

During Mc Cawley's 15-year term as Commandant, U. S. Marines staged successful landings in Panama, Chile, Egypt, Korea, Haiti, Samoa, Argentina, Japan, and the Hawaiian Is. to protect American lives and property. Marines also served in Alaska where they patrolled the Bering shores to eliminate seal poaching.

Colonel Mc Cawley retired from active service at the age of 64 on January 29, 1891. He died in October of the same year at Rosemont, Pa., and his remains were buried in the Old Churchyard at Abbington, Pa.

CHARLES HEYWOOD

NINTH COMMANDANT
June 30, 1891, to October 2, 1903

b. In Maine, October 3, 1839;
d. Washington, D. C., February 26, 1915

CHARLES HEYWOOD was appointed a second lieutenant in the Marine Corps on April 5, 1858. During that year he was stationed at the MB Washington, D.C., and at Brooklyn, N.Y. While on duty in Brooklyn he served in the Quarantine riots at Staten Island, N.Y. He performed special duty on the *Niagara,* and later on board the *St. Louis* of the Home Squadron, the ship seeking filibusters in Central America.

He was invalided from Aspinwall (Colon) in January 1860, and later was ordered to the sloop of war *Cumberland,* flagship of the Squadron of Observation at Vera Cruz, Mexico. In March 1861, he returned to duty on board the *Cumberland* and with that vessel took part in the destruction of the Norfolk Navy Yard during the Civil War.

In May 1861, Heywood was promoted to first lieutenant and

landed with the Marines at Hatteras Inlet, where he was present at the capture of Forts Clark and Hatteras. He was advanced to captain in November of that year, and during the winter of 1861-62, participated actively in a number of boat expeditions in the James River.

In the fight between the *Cumberland* and the *Merrimac* in March 1862, his conduct was particularly noteworthy while commanding the after gun deck division, firing the last gun in the fight and saving himself by jumping overboard as the *Cumberland* went down with her flag still flying. He was favorably mentioned for his gallant conduct and received the brevet rank of major for his services during the engagement. For some time afterward, both on shore and at sea, he was actively engaged in the search for the notorious raider *Alabama,* until he applied for duty on board the flagship *Hartford.* He was ordered to that vessel as Fleet Marine Officer of the West Gulf Squadron.

He served on shore at Pensacola and was on board the *Hartford* in the battle of Mobile Bay, where he received the brevet rank of lieutenant colonel for gallant and meritorious services.

From 1865 to 1867, he performed duty on board various ships, serving as Admiral Farragut's Fleet Marine Officer on the European Station and later in the same capacity in the North Atlantic Squadron. During this period he also served for a time at Washington, Norfolk, and Brooklyn.

In November 1876, he attained the regular rank of major, to which he had been brevetted more than ten years before, and was ordered to command the MB, Washington, D.C. During the serious labor riots of the summer of 1877, Heywood led a battalion of Marines at Baltimore, Philadelphia, and Reading, Pa.

His next two years of duty carried him to widely separated posts —Mare Island, Calif., and Brooklyn, N.Y. In April 1885, he organized, within 24 hours from the time of the order, a battalion of 250 Marines for duty on the Isthmus of Panama to open the transit. Subsequently under his command on the Isthmus were 800 Marines in addition to a strong detachment of the U.S. Navy and the artillery.

He was promoted to lieutenant colonel on March 9, 1888, and on June 30, 1891, was appointed Colonel Commandant of the Marine Corps. By special acts of Congress he was promoted to brigadier general in March 1899, and to major general in July 1902. The energy, experience, and training which he had shown and obtained in his early days in the Marine Corps were fully evident from the moment he assumed command of the Corps. At that time the Marine Corps consisted of 75 officers and 2,100 enlisted men; but the number gradually rose during General Heywood's tenure of office until, at the time of his retirement in 1903, it had reached the total of 278 officers and 7,532 enlisted personnel.

Under his administration the number of Marine Corps posts was increased from 12 to 21. There was scarcely a regular post at which General Heywood was not able to provide new barracks or officers' quarters. He caused the regular system of target practice to be established and adopted Good Conduct Medals for the betterment of the discipline in the Marine Corps.

The declaration of war with Spain found the Marine Corps prepared. General Heywood closed a most distinguished career of more than 45 years as a commissioned officer in the Marine Corps, when on October 3, 1903, in accordance with law, having attained the age of 64 years, he was placed on the retired list. His death occurred in Washington, D.C., on February 26, 1915, and his remains were interred in the Arlington National Cemetery.

GEORGE FRANK ELLIOTT

TENTH COMMANDANT
October 3, 1903, to November 30, 1910

b. Utah, Ala., November 30, 1846;
d. Washington, D. C., November 4, 1931

AFTER attending the U. S. Military Academy for two years, George Elliott was appointed a second lieutenant in the Marine Corps on October 12, 1870. During his early career, he performed the usual round of sea and shore duty, was on field duty with the naval expedition to Panama in 1885, and guarded the legation at Seoul, Korea, after a precarious march to that city during the war between China and Japan in 1894.

During the Spanish-American War, he won considerable distinction in command of a detachment of Marines and Cubans fighting the Spaniards near Guantanamo Bay, Cuba. Later, Elliott commanded a battalion of Marines in the Battle of Novaleta during the Philippine Insurrection.

He was made Brigadier General Commandant of the Marine Corps on October 3, 1903, but left his headquarters shortly afterward and took personal command of a brigade of Marines maintaining order in Panama shortly after that country gained its independence.

During his tenure as Commandant he raised the educational requirements for officers, instituted an improved system of rifle firing and, by his untiring efforts, obtained stronger support from Congress for the Corps. By his skillful maneuvering of a delicate situation he succeeded in having Marines reassigned to vessels of the Navy from which they had been removed by order of President Theodore Roosevelt.

Elliott retired from the Corps with the rank of major general on November 30, 1910.

He died in Washington, D.C., on November 4, 1931.

WILLIAM P. BIDDLE

ELEVENTH COMMANDANT
February 3, 1911, to February 24, 1914

b. Philadelphia, Pa., December 15, 1853;
d. Nice, France, February 25, 1923

WILLIAM BIDDLE was commissioned a second lieutenant in the Corps in June 1875, and after short tours of duty in Washington, New York, and Philadelphia, he made the first of his many tours of sea duty. After three years aboard the USS *Hartford* and

Powhatan, he was again assigned to shore duty at Philadelphia and New York.

He returned to sea duty on the *Kearsarge* in March 1882, and was promoted to first lieutenant two years later. With a break of fewer than three years at the same domestic stations as his previous shore duty, he again went to sea for three years on board the *Swatara.* He returned to Philadelphia for duty in February 1891, where he was advanced to captain three years later.

Biddle resumed sea duty aboard the *Baltimore* in June 1895, and was shortly thereafter transferred to the *Olympia.* He served on this ship during the Spanish-American War and was with Admiral Dewey at the Battle of Manila Bay. After the close of the war, he returned to Philadelphia for duty, but was soon called to join the 4th Battalion of Marines, organized for duty in the Far East. With that battalion he arrived in China to take part in the Boxer Rebellion and in the famous relief expedition to Peking in 1900.

After the Boxer Rebellion, Biddle was transferred with his battalion to the 1st Brigade of Marines, Philippine Is., where he served for more than two years. He then returned to the States for duty at HQMC, Washington, D.C. He was advanced to lieutenant colonel on March 23, 1903, and in December of that year, he was ordered to Panama in command of the battalion of Marines on the *Dixie,* which arrived in time to participate in affairs when the independence of that country was declared.

He returned to the States soon afterward, however, and served for short tours of duty in Philadelphia and at HQMC. He was promoted to colonel in February 1905, and during the following year, returned to the Philippine Is., where he commanded the 1st Brigade of Marines for approximately two years. He reported for duty at HQMC in May 1908, and was soon assigned command of an expeditionary brigade, organized in Philadelphia, for service in Panama to reinforce the troops protecting the construction of the Panama Canal, and for potential duty in Nicaragua.

Biddle returned to HQ in April 1910. During the closing months of General Elliott's term as Commandant, General Biddle acted as Commandant of the Marine Corps most of the time. He was appointed Commandant of the Corps on February 3, 1911.

His tour of duty as the 11th Commandant was a comparatively short, quiet, and uneventful one. He concerned himself primarily with the routine affairs of the Marine Corps. Under his tenure, several minor expeditions took place, including the first intervention in Nicaragua.

Following approximately three years in office, General Biddle applied for retirement on the ground of having completed more than 30 years' service, and he was retired on February 24, 1914. He was recalled to active duty during World War I and served primarily on court-martial duty in San Diego, Calif. His death occurred in Nice, France, in 1923.

GEORGE BARNETT

TWELFTH COMMANDANT
February 25, 1914, to June 30, 1920

b. Lancaster, Wis., December 9, 1859;
d. Washington, D. C., April 27, 1930

GEORGE BARNETT graduated from the U.S. Naval Academy in 1881, and went to sea as a cadet-midshipman. He was commissioned a Marine second lieutenant July 1, 1883.

After serving briefly at the Brooklyn, N.Y., and Mare Island, Calif., Navy Yards, he was assigned in July 1884 to the USS *Pinta*. He was attached to that ship until August 1887, when he was ordered to the Navy Yard, Washington, D.C. In April 1888, he entered the torpedo school at Newport, R.I., returning to Washington in August of the same year. After brief tours of duty at the Washington Navy Yard and the Marine Barracks, Washington, he joined the Marine Detachment of the USS *Iroquois* in May 1889.

Barnett returned to the Washington Navy Yard in May 1892, and was temporarily detached to the Marine Guard at the Columbian Exposition in Chicago from May to December 1893. He completed his Washington tour in March 1896, when he was ordered to the Marine Barracks, Portsmouth, N.H. In June 1896, he joined the Marine Detachment of the USS *Vermont* and in November 1897, was ordered to the USS *San Francisco.*

In April 1898, he was given command of the Marine Detachment of the USS *New Orleans,* serving aboard that ship throughout the Spanish-American War and participating in the shelling of Spanish forts at Santiago, Cuba. He was transferred to the USS *Chicago* in November 1898. Barnett returned to Washington in April 1901, served several months at HQMC, and in July of that year began a three-month tour of duty at Newport, R.I.

In October 1901, he was given command of the recruiting districts of western New Jersey, Delaware and Pennsylvania, with headquarters at Philadelphia. In September 1902, he assumed command of a battalion of Marines sent to Panama to protect the railroad across the Isthmus. He returned to Washington with the battalion in December 1902, and in January 1903, accompanied it to Cavite, Philippine Islands, to join the 1st Marine Brigade there. In July 1903, he was named Fleet Marine Officer of the Asiatic Fleet and commander of the Marine Detachment aboard the USS *Kentucky.*

He took command of the 1st Marine Brigade at Cavite in December 1904, returned to Washington in May 1905, and two months later assumed command of the Marine Barracks, Navy Yard, Washington, D.C.

From June to September 1906, he was stationed at the Naval War College, Newport, R.I. Barnett was again given command of an expeditionary battalion in September 1906, and accompanied the battalion to Havana, where it became part of the Cuban Army of Pacification. The expeditionary force was soon expanded to a regiment, which he also commanded. The regiment was sent to Cienfuegos, and occupied a large part of that island. When the U.S. Army relieved his unit in November 1906, General Barnett returned to Washington, resuming his command of the Marine Barracks at the Washington Navy Yard.

In November 1907, he began a brief tour of duty at HQMC, and in January 1908, was ordered to China to command the Marine Detachment at the U.S. Legation in Peking. Upon his return to the States in October 1910, he was given command of the Marine Barracks, Philadelphia. His tour of duty at Philadelphia was interrupted three times by temporary expeditionary duty to settle domestic disturbances in Cuba. He commanded the First Marine Regiment in Cuba from March to June 1911, from May to August 1912, and from February to May 1913. In December 1913, he was given the additional command of the 1st Advance Base Brigade with which he participated in the Atlantic Fleet maneuvers at Puerto Rico in January and February 1914. Upon his return from Puerto Rico, General Barnett reported to HQMC in Washington and accepted his appointment as Commandant.

Before the entry of the United States into WWI, he sent expeditionary forces to capture Vera Cruz, Mexico, in 1914, and to settle domestic disturbances in Haiti in 1915 and the Dominican Republic in 1916. In October 1920, General Barnett became the first Commanding General of the Department of the Pacific, serving in that capacity until his retirement on December 9, 1923, at the age limit of 64. He died April 27, 1930.

JOHN ARCHER LEJEUNE

THIRTEENTH COMMANDANT
July 1, 1920, to March 4, 1929

b. Pointe Coupee, La., January 10, 1867;
d. Baltimore, Md., November 20, 1942

JOHN A. LEJEUNE attended Louisiana State University, Baton Rouge, from which he was graduated with a Bachelor of Arts degree. Subsequently, he secured an appointment as a midshipman at the U.S. Naval Academy, from which he was graduated in 1888. At the expiration of a two-year cruise as a cadet midshipman, he was commissioned a second lieutenant in the Marine

Corps on July 1, 1890, and during the succeeding years, saw action in the Spanish-American War in 1898 aboard the USS *Cincinnati*.

In the fall of 1903, Lejeune, then a major, was dispatched to Panama with a battalion of Marines when conditions became critical in the revolution in Colombia.

He returned to Panama three years later, following a brief tour of duty at the MB in Washington, D.C., During the following years he was transferred to duty in the Philippines, arriving in May 1907. While there he commanded the Marine Barracks, Navy Yard, Cavite, and later the 1st Brigade of Marines. He was detached to the States in June 1909.

His next tour of foreign shore duty was served in Cuba with the 2nd Provisional Brigade Marines from May 1912 to December of the same year. After a short period in the States, he was again detached to expeditionary service in Cuba in February 1913, this time with the 2nd Brigade at Guantanamo Bay. In November 1913, he sailed from New York with the Second Advance Base Regiment, his ultimate destination Vera Cruz, Mexico, where he landed with his unit in April of 1914. He returned home in December 1914, this time reporting to HQMC in Washington, D.C., to become assistant to the Major General Commandant of the Marine Corps.

With the outbreak of WWI, Lejeune assumed command of the newly constructed MB at Quantico, Va. Overseas service was, however, inevitable, and in June 1918, he arrived at Brest, France. Upon reporting to the commander of the AEF, he was assigned to command a brigade of the 32nd Division, and assumed command of the 4th Brigade of Marines of the Second Division immediately following the attack of that division in the Soissons offensive. On July 28, 1918, General Lejeune assumed command of the Second Division and remained in that capacity until August 1919, when the unit was demobilized. He was the first Marine officer to hold an Army divisional command, and following the Armistice, he led his division in the march into Germany.

During WWI he was recognized by the French government as a strategist and leader, receiving the Legion of Honor and the Croix de Guerre from that country. In October 1919, he again was appointed Commanding General, Marine Barracks, Quantico, prior to his appointment as Major General Commandant of the Marine Corps on June 30, 1920.

Upon the expiration of his second term as Commandant, General Lejeune, although reluctant to retire from the Marine Corps, declined reappointment on March 4, 1929, and on November 12, 1929, he retired in order to accept the position of superintendent of the Virginia Military Institute, serving there until poor health necessitated his resignation in October 1937.

In February 1942, he was advanced to the rank of lieutenant general on the Marine Corps retired list. General Lejeune died on November 20, 1942, at the Union Memorial Hospital, Baltimore, Md., and was interred in Arlington National Cemetery with full military honors. Today, Camp Lejeune, N.C., bears the name of one of the ablest officers of the American military forces, and one of the most distinguished soldiers of World War I.

WENDELL CUSHING NEVILLE

FOURTEENTH COMMANDANT
March 5, 1929, to July 8, 1930

b. Portsmouth, Va., May 12, 1870;
d. Edgewater Beach, Md., July 8, 1930

W ENDELL C. NEVILLE entered the U.S. Naval Academy at Annapolis, Md., in 1886. He received his diploma in 1890 and, following a two-year cruise aboard a warship, was commissioned a second lieutenant in the Marine Corps.

At the outbreak of the Spanish-American War, Lieutenant Neville was assigned to the 1st Marine Battalion, hurriedly organized under Lieutenant Colonel W. R. Huntington for service in Cuba. The battalion staged an attack under heavy gunfire at Guantanamo Bay, established a beachhead and routed enemy forces in that area. For outstanding valor and leadership in that action,

Lieutenant Neville was awarded the Brevet Medal, and was promoted to the brevet rank of captain.

Promoted to the permanent rank of captain a few months after the war, he was assigned to a battalion of Marines ordered to China to relieve the hard-pressed garrison at Peking during the Boxer Rebellion. He took part in four battles in that area and was again commended for his gallantry.

In the Philippine Islands not long afterward, he was appointed military governor of Basilan Province. Following that assignment he served in Cuba, Nicaragua, Panama, and Hawaii. While in command of Marines landing at Vera Cruz on April 21, 1914, he displayed conspicuous gallantry. In that operation, Lieutenant Colonel Neville was awarded the Medal of Honor for his distinguished conduct.

Prior to his embarkation for France in 1917, Colonel Neville returned to China where he was chosen to command the combined Allied guard at Peking. On January 1, 1918, he was placed in command of the Fifth Marine Regiment in France, and in May moved his regiment into action at Belleau Wood where Germany's big drive was decisively halted.

In July, General Neville was appointed brigade commander, responsible for the 4th Marine Brigade which he directed during the remaining days of the war and during its occupation service in Germany. After service with the Army of Occupation in Germany, General Neville and his brigade returned to the States in July 1919.

Promoted to major general in March 1920, he served as assistant to the CMC and later became CG, Department of the Pacific, with headquarters in San Francisco. Prior to becoming Commandant on March 5, 1929, he was in command of the MB, Quantico, Va. General Neville's sudden death on July 8, 1930, while in office as Major General Commandant, closed one of the most brilliant military careers of his day.

BEN HEBARD FULLER

FIFTEENTH COMMANDANT
August 6, 1930, to February 28, 1934

b. Big Rapids, Mich., February 27, 1870;
d. Washington, D. C., June 8, 1937

Ben FULLER, whose active service in the Corps totaled 48 years, nine months and eight days, entered the U.S. Naval Academy in May 1885. After finishing the four-year course of instruction, he was assigned to the prescribed two-year cruise as a naval cadet on various vessels of the Pacific Squadron. He was commissioned a second lieutenant in the Marine Corps on July 1, 1891, with six other members of his graduating class. Together with his Marine classmates, he took the first course ever given for Marine officers in the School of Application at the MB, Washington, D.C., from which he graduated in March of the following year.

His military education continued in the following years with courses of instruction at Fort Leavenworth, the Army War College, and the Navy War College. Fuller's first three years of service in the Marine Corps were spent ashore at various posts in the eastern part of the States. On September 7, 1893, he was promoted to first lieutenant and then went to sea for the first time as a Marine officer on the USS *Atlanta* in April of the next year.

During his active career he spent nearly seven years aboard a dozen different naval vessels. During the Spanish-American War he was in command of the Marine detachment of the USS *Columbia* and served in West Indian waters. Shortly after that war he was promoted to captain and transferred to the Philippines for duty, where he participated in the Battle of Novaleta.

At the outbreak of the Boxer Rebellion in 1900, he was placed in command of a company of artillery in an expeditionary Marine force. He participated in the siege and capture of Tientsin and was commended in Navy General Orders for his "gallant, meritorious and courageous conduct" in battle. He joined in the march of the relief column to Peking and was in command of an independent detachment at Fong Chow, China.

Captain Fuller returned to the Philippines in October 1900, and went to the States the following year. During the next three years he was given several peacetime shore assignments, and spent a few months at sea. He was promoted to major in March 1904. Shortly thereafter he was transferred to the command of Marine Barracks, Honolulu, T.H., where he served for about two years, then went to New York for duty.

After a brief tour of duty in the States, a part of which was spent as instructor in the School of Application at Annapolis, he again served on foreign duty—this time to the Canal Zone where he served as commanding officer of the battalion of Marines from August 1908 until February 1910. His next regular station of duty was in command of the Marine Barracks at Charleston, S.C. He was promoted to lieutenant colonel March 8, 1911. While serving at Charleston he commanded a regiment of an expeditionary brigade of Marines that went to Guantanamo Bay, Cuba, in May 1911.

He spent most of the next two years in service schools. Fuller joined the Fifth Regiment of Marines as second in command in July 1914, and spent several months with that organization on the *Hancock,* cruising around Haiti-Santo Domingo and in camp at Guantanamo Bay.

Some two years later, after a short cruise as Fleet Marine Officer, Atlantic Fleet, and while attending the Navy War College, he was promoted to colonel in March 1917. He commanded the Marine Barracks, Philadelphia, Pa., for about one year, beginning early in September 1917, and was then assigned to the command of the 2nd Provisional Brigade of Marines engaged in a military occupation of Santo Domingo.

He was promoted to temporary brigadier general in August 1918, but reverted to his regular rank of colonel about one year later. While serving in Santo Domingo he had extensive experience in administering several cabinet positions in the military government of that country. He joined the staff of the Naval War College as an instructor in November 1920, and in July 1922, took command of the Marine Corps Schools at Quantico, which position he held for the next year and a half. Next, Fuller was assigned to command the 1st Brigade of Marines occupying Haiti in January 1924, until December 1925.

He was promoted to the regular rank of brigadier general as of February 8, 1924. During the next two and a half years he spent most of the time serving in Washington, D.C. He was made Assistant Commandant of the Corps in July 1928, under Major General Lejeune, and continued to serve in that capacity, not only during the remainder of Lejeune's tenure of office, but also throughout that of General Neville. During General Neville's brief period as Major General Commandant in 1929-1930, General Fuller frequently acted as Commandant when Neville was ill.

After the death of General Neville, Fuller was selected as Major General Commandant on August 6, 1930. General Fuller's tenure as Commandant of the Marine Corps was one of general retrenchment due to the world-wide depression, the initiation of the good-neighbor policy in dealing with Latin American countries, and other reasons. The depression brought about a sharp reduction in the federal revenue, and in an effort to offset this, appropriations for the Marine Corps were reduced and the curtailments were offset by reductions in the enlisted strength, and a flat reduction in pay. However, two years later, sweeping changes in foreign policy caused the Marine Corps to redefine its mission in the scheme of national defense. The necessity for a substantial expeditionary force of Marines to be in readiness to accompany the Fleet was an idea that had taken form not long after the turn of the century, but it was not until 1933, when personnel became available as a result of withdrawal of Marines from foreign countries, that the idea was fully developed and such a force as the Fleet Marine Force was organized. That organization came into being in December of that year, with part of its force at Quantico, Va., and a portion at San Diego, Calif.

The gradual expansion of the Navy during Fuller's tenure of office demanded more and more Marines for sea duty. This, together with the further development of the Fleet Marine Force, influenced the development of the Corps' amphibious doctrines.

General Fuller was transferred to the retired list of the Marine Corps on March 1, 1934, after having attained the statutory age limit of 64 years. He died in Washington, D.C., on June 8, 1937.

JOHN HENRY RUSSELL, JR.

SIXTEENTH COMMANDANT
April 5, 1934, to November 30, 1936

b. Mare Island, Calif., November 14, 1872;
d. Coronado, Calif., March 6, 1947

J OHN RUSSELL entered the Naval Academy at Annapolis in May 1888. He graduated with the class of 1892 and, after two years as a naval cadet, he was commissioned a second lieutenant in the Marine Corps on July 1, 1894. He served at shore stations until June 1, 1896, then went aboard the *USS Massachusetts.*

During the Spanish-American War he served on that ship in the blockading operations around the West Indies and in the bombardment of the forts of Santiago, Cuba. In November 1898, he was promoted to first lieutenant and was assigned, in turn, to Philadelphia, Norfolk and Washington, D.C. He was promoted to captain on March 28, 1899, while serving aboard the *USS Yosemite.*

Duty followed on Guam, in the States at East Coast stations and at Mare Island, Calif., and aboard the *USS Oregon.* He was promoted to major in July 1906, and transferred to the command of the Marine Barracks, Honolulu, Hawaii. From Hawaii his duty assignments took him to the Canal Zone, back to the States on the staff of the Navy War College, to the legation guard at Peking, China, then to Washington, D.C. and Office of Naval Intelligence.

Early in 1914, he was given command of the 2nd Battalion, Third Marines, and landed with that unit at Vera Cruz, Mexico, on April 30, 1914. The battalion remained in Mexico until December, when it was withdrawn, and Major Russell returned to his regular assignment with the Navy Department. He was promoted to lieutenant colonel and took command of the 1st Provisional Brigade of Marines occupying Haiti.

During his tour of duty in Haiti he became thoroughly familiar with its political and economic difficulties and, on February 11, 1922, after promotion to brigadier general, he was appointed as High Commissioner of Haiti with the rank of Ambassador Extraordinary. He remained in this important assignment for nearly nine years before being transferred to San Diego, where he took command in November 1930. A year later he was assigned to Quantico, and from there he returned to HQMC as Assistant to the Commandant.

He was promoted to major general and continued as Assistant to the CMC until he was appointed Commandant on April 5, 1934. His administration lasted only two years and eight months, but it brought significant changes and progress within the Corps. General Russell reached the statutory age limit in November 1936, and was retired from active duty on December 1, 1936. He died in Coronado, Calif., on March 6, 1947.

THOMAS HOLCOMB

SEVENTEENTH COMMANDANT
December 1, 1936, to December 31, 1943

b. New Castle, Del., August 5, 1879;
d. New Castle, Del., May 24, 1965

THOMAS HOLCOMB was educated in Delaware and in Washington, D.C. He was appointed a second lieutenant from civil life on April 13, 1900. Holcomb was on detached duty with a company of Marines, organized for service with a Marine battalion, attached to the North Atlantic Fleet, from September 1902 to April 1903, and he served in the Philippine Islands from April 1904 to August 1905, and from October to November 1906.

Holcomb was on duty with the Legation Guard, Peking, China, from September 1905 to September 1906, and again from December 1908 to July 1910, being then detached from the Legation Guard. On May 13, 1908, he was promoted to captain and continued on duty in Peking as Attache on the staff of the American Minister for study of the Chinese language. He remained on that duty until May 1911.

In December 1911, he was again ordered to the Legation at Peking to continue his study of the Chinese language, and remained there until May 1914. Holcomb has been prominently identified with the development of rifle shooting, and served as Inspector of Target Practice in the Marine Corps from October 1914 to August 1917. In addition, he was a member of the Marine Corps Rifle Teams of 1901, 1902, 1903, 1907, 1908, and 1911, and of teams representing the United States in the Palma Trophy Match in 1902 and 1903.

On August 29, 1916, he was promoted to major. From August 1917, to January 1918, he commanded the 2d Battalion, Sixth Regiment, at Marine Barracks, Quantico, in preparation for overseas service. From February 1918 to July 1919, he served with the AEF in France, in command of the 2d Battalion until August 1918, and thereafter as second in command of the Sixth Regiment. He participated in all engagements in which the Regiment took part —the Aisne defensive (Chateau-Thierry); the Aisne-Marne offensive (Soissons); the Marbache sector; the St. Mihiel offensive; the Meuse-Argonne (Champagne) offensive; the Meuse-Argonne (Argonne Forest) offensive; and the march to the Rhine in Germany following the Armistice.

He was promoted to lieutenant colonel on June 4, 1920. In recognition of his distinguished services he was awarded the Navy Cross, the Silver Star with three Oak Leaf Clusters, a Meritorious Service Citation by the Commander-in-Chief, AEF, the Purple

Heart, and was three times cited in General Orders of the Second Division, AEF. The French government conferred on him the Cross of the Legion of Honor, and three times awarded him the Croix de Guerre with Palm. From September 1922 to June 1924, he commanded the Marine Barracks, Naval Station, Guantanamo Bay, Cuba, and on his return to the States, was ordered to the Command and General Staff School of the Army at Fort Leavenworth, completing the course as a Distinguished Graduate in June 1925. He was then ordered to HQMC for duty in the Division of Operations and Training, where he remained until June 1927.

On December 22, 1928, he was promoted to colonel. From August 1927 to February 1930, Colonel Holcomb commanded the Marine Detachment, American Legation, Peiping, China. In June 1930, he went to the Naval War College as a student, Senior Course, from which he graduated in June 1931. He was then ordered to the Army War College, from which course he graduated in June 1932.

From June 1932 to January 1935, Holcomb served in the Office of Naval Operations, Navy Department. He was promoted to brigadier general on February 1, 1935. He then served as Commandant of the MCS in Quantico until November 1936, when he was ordered to HQMC to assume the office of Major General Commandant on December 1, 1936.

During his tenure he expanded the organization from 15,000 to 305,000 fighting men. On December 1, 1940, he was reappointed Major General Commandant for four years by the President. With his advancement to lieutenant general on January 20, 1942, General Holcomb became the highest ranking officer ever to command the Corps. Upon retiring as Marine Corps Commandant on January 1, 1944, General Holcomb was placed on the retired list, raised to full general, and then ordered to active duty. After more than 40 years of service, he went off the active rolls of the Marine Corps on April 10, 1944.

ALEXANDER ARCHER VANDEGRIFT

EIGHTEENTH COMMANDANT
January 1, 1944, to December 31, 1947

b. Charlottesville, Va., March 13, 1887
d. Bethesda, Md., May 8, 1973

ALEXANDER VANDEGRIFT attended the University of Virginia and was commissioned in the Marine Corps as a second lieutenant on January 22, 1909. Following instruction at the Marine Officers' School, Port Royal, S.C., and a tour of duty at the MB, Portsmouth, N.H., he went to foreign shore duty in the Caribbean area where he participated in the bombardment, assault, and capture of Coyotepe in Nicaragua. He further participated in the engagement and occupation of Vera Cruz, Mexico.

In December 1914, Vandegrift attended the Advance Base Course at the MB, Philadelphia. Upon completion of schooling, he sailed for Haiti with the 1st Brigade and participated in action against hostile Cacos bandits at Le Trou and Fort Capois. In August 1916, he became a member of the Haitian Constabulary, Port au Prince, where he remained until detached to the States in December 1918.

He returned to Haiti again in July 1919 to serve with the Gendarmerie d'Haiti as an Inspector of Constabulary. He returned to the States in April 1923, and was assigned to the MB at Quantico. He completed the Field Officers' Course, MCS, in May 1926, after which he went to the MCB, San Diego, Calif. as Assistant Chief of Staff.

In February 1927, he sailed for China where he served as Operations and Training Officer of the 3rd Marine Brigade with HQ at Tientsin. He was ordered to Washington, D.C., in September 1928, where he became Assistant Chief Coordinator, Bureau of the Budget. Following duty in Washington, he joined the MB, Quantico, where he became Assistant Chief of Staff, G-1 Section, FMF, in which post he remained until ordered to China in June 1935. Here he was successively Executive Officer and CO of the Marine Detachment at the American Embassy in Peiping.

He reported to HQMC, Washington, D.C., in June 1937, where he became Military Secretary to the Major General Commandant. In March 1940, he was appointed Assistant to the Major General Commandant, in which position he remained until November 1941, when he was detached to the First Marine Division. General Vandegrift sailed with the division as CG in May 1942 for the south Pacific, where on August 7, 1942, in the Solomon Is., he led ashore the First Marine Division (Reinf.), in the first large-scale offensive action against the Japanese.

In July 1943, he assumed command of the I Marine Amphibious Corps and commanded this organization in the landing at Empress Augusta Bay, Bougainville, northern Solomon Is., on November 1, 1943. Upon establishing the initial beachhead, he relinquished command and returned to HQMC, where on January 1, 1944, he became Commandant of the Marine Corps.

His first gigantic task was the chore of building the Marine Corps to meet the demands of the two years to follow. Under "Archie" Vandegrift's cool, tenacious direction, the Corps was increased by another 125,000 men. At war's end, General Vandegrift was faced with the twin tasks of demobilization and the establishment of the Marine Corps on a permanent post-war basis, commensurate with the needs and demands which might arise in the future. General Vandegrift left active service on December 31, 1947. He was placed on the retired list April 1, 1949. His death occurred at Bethesda, Md., on May 8, 1973.

CLIFTON BLEDSOE CATES

NINETEENTH COMMANDANT
January 1, 1948, to December 31, 1951

b. Tiptonville, Tenn., August 31, 1893
d. Annapolis, Md., June 4, 1970

C LIFTON CATES attended the Missouri Military Academy where

he became an honor student and a four-letter man in sports. His Bachelor of Laws degree was obtained at the University of Tennessee in 1916. On June 13, 1917, as a reserve second lieutenant, he reported for active duty at Marine Barracks, Port Royal, S.C., and sailed for France the following January.

With the Sixth Marine Regiment in WWI, Cates fought in the Verdun defensive sector; at Bouresches and Belleau Wood in the Aisne defensive; at Soissons in the Aisne-Marne offensive; in the Marbache sector of the St.-Mihiel offensive; and in the Mont Blanc and Argonne-Forest engagements of the Meuse-Argonne offensive.

He earned the Navy Cross, Army Distinguished Service Cross, and an Oak Leaf Cluster in lieu of a second Distinguished Service Cross for heroism in the Bouresches and Belleau Wood fighting, where he was both gassed and wounded. He was awarded the Silver Star Medal at Soissons, where he was wounded a second time, and an Oak Leaf Cluster in lieu of a second Silver Star Medal in the Mont Blanc fighting. Apart from those decorations, the French government recognized his heroism with the Legion of Honor and the Croix de Guerre with Gilt Star and two palms.

After participating in the occupation of Germany. Cates returned to the States in September 1919, and during the next year served in Washington, D.C., as a White House aide and aide-de-camp to the Commandant of the Marine Corps. He then served at San Francisco, Calif., as aide-de-camp to the CG, Department of the Pacific, from October 1920 until June 1923, when he began a tour of sea duty as commander of the Marine Detachment aboard the USS *California*. That assignment was completed in April 1925. A month later he began a year of service with the Fourth Marine Regiment at San Diego, Calif.

In March 1928, after serving on recruiting duty at Spokane, Wash., and Omaha, Neb., he was named a member of the American Battle Monuments Commission at Washington. He served in that capacity until May 1929, then was ordered to Shanghai, China, where he rejoined the Fourth Marines. Three years later he was detached from that regiment to return to Washington for study in the Army Industrial College. Completing his course in June 1933, he reported the following month to Quantico, where he served with the Seventh Marines and completed the Senior Course in the MCS.

He returned again to Washington in September 1935, and was assigned to the War Plans Section of the Division of Operations and Training at HQMC. In August 1937, Cates sailed for Shanghai as a battalion commander with the Sixth Marine Regiment, serving with that unit until he rejoined the Fourth Marines in March 1938. Again the following year he was brought back to Washington for instruction in the Army War College. That course was completed in June 1940, and he reported the next month to the Philadelphia Navy Yard as director of the Marine Officers' Basic School.

By the time the United States entered WWII, he had been promoted to colonel. In May 1942, Colonel Cates took command of the First Marine Regiment which, as part of the First Marine Division, he led at Guadalcanal. With the invaluable experience obtained in that campaign, he was returned to the States the following March for his first tour of duty as Commandant of the MCS at Quantico. He continued in that capacity until June 1944. The following month he took command of the Fourth Marine Division, leading that organization in the Pacific theater until the end of the war. Meanwhile, he had been promoted to major general.

Ordered back to the States in December 1945, the general became President of the Marine Corps Equipment Board at Quantico, holding that position for six months before he was named CG of the Marine Barracks, Quantico. He held that command until January 1, 1948, when he was advanced to the rank of general and sworn in as Commandant of the Marine Corps. When he completed his four-year term as Commandant, he reverted to the rank of lieutenant general and began his second tour as Commandant of the MCS. He was again promoted to general upon his retirement on June 30, 1954. General Cates died at Annapolis, Md., on June 4, 1970.

LEMUEL CORNICK SHEPHERD, JR.

TWENTIETH COMMANDANT
January 1, 1952, to December 31, 1955

b. Norfolk, Va., February 10, 1896

Lemuel C. Shepherd, a graduate of Virginia Military Institute, was commissioned a second lieutenant in the Marine Corps on April 11, 1917. On May 19, he reported for active duty at the Marine Barracks, Port Royal, S.C. Less than a month later, he sailed for France as a member of the Fifth Marine Regiment with the first elements of the AEF. He served in defensive sectors in the vicinity of Verdun and participated in the Aisne-Marne offensive (Chateau-Thierry) where he was twice wounded in action at Belleau Wood during the fighting there in June 1918.

Upon returning to the front in August, he rejoined the Fifth Marines and saw action in the St. Mihiel and Meuse-Argonne (Champagne) offensive where he was wounded for the third time. For his gallantry in action at Belleau Wood, Lieutenant Shepherd was awarded the Army Distinguished Service Cross, the Navy Cross, the French Croix de Guerre, and was cited in the general orders of the Second Infantry Division, AEF.

After duty with the Army of Occupation in Germany, Shepherd sailed for home in July 1919. In September, he returned to France for duty in connection with the preparation of relief maps of the battlefields over which the 4th Brigade of Marines had fought. Upon Shepherd's return to the States in December 1920, he was assigned as Aide-de-Camp to the Commandant and Aide at the White House. In July 1922, he was assigned duty in command of a selected company of Marines at the Brazilian Exposition at Rio de Janeiro. In June of 1923, he was ordered to sea duty as commanding officer of the Marine Detachment aboard the USS *Idaho*. This tour was followed by duty at the MB, Norfolk, Va., where he commanded the Sea School.

In April 1927, he sailed for expeditionary duty in China, where he served in the 3rd Marine Brigade in Tientsin and Shanghai. Upon returning to the States in 1929, he attended the Field Officers' Course, Marine Corps Schools. After graduation, Captain Shepherd was assigned to overseas duty again, this time on detached duty with the Garde d'Haiti, where he served for four years as a District and Department Commander.

Following the withdrawal of Marines from Haiti in 1934, Shepherd, then a major, was detailed to the Marine Barracks, Washington, D.C., as Executive Officer and as Registrar of the Marine Corps Institute. Promoted to lieutenant colonel in 1936, he was assigned to the Naval War College at Newport, R.I. Following graduation in May 1937, he commanded the 2nd Battalion, Fifth Marine Regiment, part of the newly formed FMF, Atlantic, which was being extensively employed in the development of amphibious tactics and techniques. In June 1939, he was ordered to the staff of the MCS, Quantico, Va., where he served during the next three years as Director, Correspondence School; Chief of the Tactical Section; Officer in Charge of the Candidates Class; and Assistant Commandant.

In March 1942, four months after the United States' entry into WWII, Colonel Shepherd was ordered to command the Ninth Marine Regiment. He organized, trained, and took this unit overseas as part of the Third Marine Division. Upon appointment to flag rank in July 1943, while serving on Guadalcanal, Brigadier General Shepherd was assigned as Assistant Division Commander of the First Marine Division. In this capacity, he participated in the Cape Gloucester operation on New Britain from December 1943 through March 1944, where he was awarded a Legion of Merit for distinguished service in command of the operations in the Borgen Bay area.

In May 1944, General Shepherd assumed command of the 1st Provisional Marine Brigade and led this organization in the invasion and subsequent recapture of Guam during July and August of 1944. For distinguished leadership in this operation, General Shepherd received his first Distinguished Service Medal, and was promoted to major general. After organizing the Sixth Marine Division from the Brigade, Major General Shepherd commanded it throughout the Okinawa Operation and subsequently took that unit to Tsingtao, China. There, on October 25, 1945, he received the surrender of the Japanese forces in this area. For exceptionally meritorious service as Commanding General of the Sixth Marine Division, in the assault and occupation of Okinawa (April 1 to June 21, 1945), he was awarded a Gold Star in lieu of a second Distinguished Service Medal.

Several months later, the general returned to the States and in March 1946, organized the Troop Training Command, Amphibious Forces, Atlantic Fleet, at Little Creek, Va. On November 1 of the same year, he was ordered to duty as Assistant to the Commandant and Chief of Staff of HQMC. He remained at this post until April 1948, when he was assigned to Quantico, where he served as Commandant of the Marine Corps Schools until June 1950.

When the Korean War erupted, General Shepherd was in command of the FMF, Pacific, with HQ at Pearl Harbor. In this capacity, he participated in the landing at Inchon and the evacuation of our forces from Hungnam following the withdrawal from the Chosin Reservoir in North Korea in December 1950.

On January 1, 1952, he was appointed Commandant of the Marine Corps by the President of the United States. During General Shepherd's four-year tenure as the 20th Commandant, he initiated a number of important policies which resulted in an increased military proficiency of the Corps. He was the first Commandant to become a member of the Joint Chiefs of Staff, and upon his retirement on January 1, 1956, he was awarded a third Distinguished Service Medal. Two months after his retirement, General Shepherd was recalled to active duty and appointed Chairman of the Inter-American Defense Board.

RANDOLPH McCALL PATE

TWENTY-FIRST COMMANDANT
January 1, 1956, to December 31, 1959

b. Port Royal, S. C., February 11, 1898;
d. Bethesda, Md., July 31, 1961

RANDOLPH MCCALL PATE served with the U. S. Army in 1918, then entered the Virginia Military Institute, graduating in June 1921. He was commissioned a second lieutenant in the Marine Corps Reserve that September, and the following May accepted his commission in the Regular Marine Corps.

In addition to expeditionary duty in Santo Domingo in 1923 and 1924, and in China from 1927 to 1929, Pate served at various posts in the States and Hawaii. He was promoted to first lieutenant in September 1926, to captain in November 1934, and to major in October 1938.

In the spring of 1939, he became Assistant Chief of Staff for Supply, First Marine Division, at New River (later Camp Lejeune), and while there was promoted to lieutenant colonel in January 1942. He began his World War II service in this capacity, participating in the planning and combat phases of the Guadalcanal campaign. He was promoted to colonel in December 1943, and later saw further service in the Pacific area.

Returning to the States after the war, he was named Director of the Division of Reserve at Marine Corps Headquarters in January 1946. The following year he assumed duties as a member of the General Board, Navy Department, Washington. In July 1948, he became Chief of Staff of the Marine Corps Schools, Quantico, Va., and two years later, was named Director of the Marine Corps Educational Center. While stationed at Quantico in September 1949, he was promoted to brigadier general.

In July 1951, General Pate was assigned to the Office of the Joint Chiefs of Staff, where he served as Deputy Director of the Joint Staff, for logistic plans. He was named Director of the

Marine Corps Reserve for a second time that November, and in August 1952, was promoted to major general. The following month, he took command of the Second Marine Division at Camp Lejeune. Ordered to Korea in June 1953, he commanded the First Marine Division until May 1954.

In July 1954, the general was appointed Assistant Commandant of the Marine Corps and Chief of Staff with the rank of lieutenant general for eighteen months. On January 1, 1956, he was promoted to the rank of general and executed the oath of office as Commandant of the Marine Corps, succeeding General Lemuel C. Shepherd. Following four years as Commandant, he retired with the rank of general.

Following a brief illness, General Pate died at the U. S. Naval Hospital, Bethesda, Md., July 31, 1961. On August 3rd, the general was interred with full military honors in Arlington National Cemetery.

DAVID MONROE SHOUP

TWENTY-SECOND COMMANDANT
January 1, 1960, to December 31, 1963

b. Battle Ground, Ind., December 30, 1904

DAVID SHOUP graduated from DePauw University, where he was a member of the ROTC. He served for a month as a second lieutenant in the Army Infantry Reserve before he was commissioned a Marine second lieutenant on July 20, 1926. Ordered to Marine Officers' Basic School at the Philadelphia Navy Yard, Lieutenant Shoup's instruction was interrupted twice by temporary duty elsewhere in the States, and by expeditionary duty with the Sixth Marines in Tientsin, China. After serving in China during most of 1927, he completed Basic School in 1928. He then served at Quantico, Va., Pensacola, Fla., and San Diego, Calif. From June 1929, to September 1931, Lieutenant Shoup was assigned to the Marine Detachment aboard the USS *Maryland*. By coincidence, the *Maryland* was the flagship for the assault on Tarawa where he earned the Medal of Honor 12 years later—providing emergency naval gunfire support with her 16-inch guns early on D-Day.

On his return from sea duty, Shoup served as a company officer at the MCB (later Marine Corps Recruit Depot), San Diego, until May 1932, when he was ordered to the Puget Sound Navy Yard, Bremerton, Wash. He was promoted to first lieutenant in June 1932. Lieutenant Shoup later served on temporary duty with the Civilian Conservation Corps in Idaho and New Jersey from June 1933 to May 1934.

Following duty in Seattle, Wash., he was again ordered to China in November 1934, serving briefly with the Fourth Marines in Shanghai and, subsequently, at the American Legation in Peiping. He returned to the States, via Japan, early in June 1936, and was again stationed at the Puget Sound Navy Yard.

He was promoted to captain in October 1936. Captain Shoup entered the Junior Course, Marine Corps Schools, Quantico, in July 1937. On completing the course in May 1938, he served as an instructor for two years.

In June 1940, he joined the Sixth Marines in San Diego. He was promoted to major in April 1941. One month later, Major Shoup was ordered to Iceland with the Sixth Marines and, after serving as Regimental Operations Officer, became Operations Officer of the 1st Marine Brigade in Iceland in October 1941.

For the service he rendered in Iceland during the first three months after the United States entered World War II, he was awarded the Letter of Commendation with Commendation Ribbon. He assumed command of the 2nd Bn., Sixth Marines, in February 1942. On returning to the States in March, the 1st Marine Brigade was disbanded and he returned with his battalion to San Diego.

In July 1942, he became Assistant Operations and Training Officer of the Second Marine Division. He was promoted to lieutenant colonel in August 1942. Sailing from San Diego aboard the USS *Matsonia* in September 1942, Lieutenant Colonel Shoup arrived in Wellington, New Zealand, later that month. From then until November 1943, he served as G-3, Operations and Training Officer of the Second Marine Division during its training period in New Zealand. His service in this capacity during the planning of the assault on Tarawa earned him his first Legion of Merit with Combat "V."

During this period he also served briefly as an observer with the First Marine Division on Guadalcanal in October 1942, and with the 43rd Army Division on Rendova, New Georgia, earning a Purple Heart in the later operation.

Promoted to colonel, November 9, 1943, Colonel Shoup was placed in command of the Second Marines, the spearhead of the assault on Tarawa. During this action he earned the Medal of Honor as well as a second Purple Heart. In December 1943, he became Chief of Staff of the Second Marine Division. For outstanding service in this capacity from June to August 1944, he was again awarded the Legion of Merit with Combat "V." He returned to the States in October 1944.

On his return, Colonel Shoup served as Logistics Officer, Division of Plans and Policies, HQMC. He was again ordered overseas in June 1947. Two months later he became commanding officer, Service Command, FMF, Pacific.

In June 1949, he joined the First Marine Division at Camp Pendleton as Division Chief of Staff. A year later he was transferred to Quantico where he served as commanding officer of the Basic School from July 1950, until April 1952.

He was then assigned to the Office of the Fiscal Director, HQMC, serving as Assistant Fiscal Director. He was promoted to brigadier general in April 1953. In July 1953, General Shoup was named Fiscal Director of the Marine Corps. While serving in this capacity, he was promoted to major general in September 1955. Subsequently, in May 1956, he began a brief assignment as Inspector General of the Marine Corps.

He returned to Camp Pendleton in June 1957, to become commanding general of the First Marine Division. General Shoup joined the Third Marine Division on Okinawa in March 1958, as commanding general. Following his return to the States, he served as commanding general of the Marine Corps Recruit Depot, Parris Island, from May to October of 1959.

On November 2, 1959, he was promoted to lieutenant general and assigned duties as Chief of Staff, HQMC. He served in this capacity until he was nominated by President Dwight D. Eisenhower to be the 22nd Commandant of the Marine Corps. Subsequently, his nomination for a four-year term, beginning January 1, 1960, was confirmed by the Senate.

After a four-year term as Commandant, General Shoup retired on December 31, 1963.

WALLACE MARTIN GREENE, JR.

TWENTY-THIRD COMMANDANT
January 1, 1964, to December 31, 1967

b. Waterbury, Vt., December 27, 1907

AFTER SCHOOLING in Burlington, Vt., and a year at the University of Vermont, Wallace Greene, Jr., entered the U.S. Naval Academy, graduating in June 1930.

As a second lieutenant, he attended the Basic School at Philadelphia, followed by duty at a number of posts and stations in the U.S., and two years aboard the *USS Tennessee*.

He joined the Fourth Marines in China in 1937. Returning in 1939, he attended the Junior Course at Quantico, Va., and subsequently served with the 1st Marine Brigade and First Marine Division.

While a Special Naval Observer in London in 1941, he attended the British Amphibious Warfare School and the Royal Engineer Demolitions School.

As Assistant Chief of Staff, G-3, for the V Amphibious Corps in 1943, then-Lieutenant Colonel Greene earned the Legion of Merit with Combat "V" for his part in the planning and execution of the Marshall Islands invasion. He received a second such award the next year, while G-3 of the Second Marine Division, for the planning of the Saipan and Tinian operations.

Duty at Headquarters Marine Corps; Little Creek, Va.; as G-3, Fleet Marine Force, Pacific; and at Quantico followed. After graduating from the National War College in 1953, he became Staff Special Assistant to the Joint Chiefs of Staff for National Security Affairs in Washington.

Appointed a brigadier general in 1955, he served as Assistant Division Commander, Second Marine Division, and in 1956 became Commanding General of the Recruit Training Command at the Marine Corps Recruit Depot, Parris Island, S.C. The next year, he took command of the Recruit Depot until assigned as Commanding General of the Marine Corps Base, Camp Lejeune, N.C.

Reporting to Headquarters Marine Corps in early 1958, General Greene served as Assistant Chief of Staff, G-3; then Deputy Chief of Staff (Plans). In January 1960, he was designated Chief of Staff at Headquarters with the rank of lieutenant general.

Nominated by President John F. Kennedy September 24, 1963, General Greene became the 23rd Commandant of the Marine Corps,, January 1, 1964, with four-star rank.

Among other medals and decorations, he holds the Distinguished Service Medal for "exceptionally meritorious service" as Chief of Staff at Marine Headquarters.

After a four-year term as Commandant, General Greene retired on December 31, 1967.

Mrs. Greene is the former Vaughan H. Emory of Fairacres, Annapolis, Md. They have a daughter, Vaughan, and a son, Wallace M. Greene, III, also a Marine officer.

LEONARD FIELDING CHAPMAN, JR.

TWENTY-FOURTH COMMANDANT
January 1, 1968, to December 31, 1971

b. Key West, Fla., November 3, 1913

Iɴ 1935, ᴡʜᴇɴ Second Lieutenant Chapman reported to the Marine Corps Officers Basic School at the Philadelphia Navy Yard, the Corps mustered 17,141 Marines, and the world was at peace. By 1969, General Chapman was serving as Commandant of a Marine Corps with an active strength of more than 317,000, committed to its third large-scale war in twenty-eight years.

In June 1935, Leonard Fielding Chapman, Jr., graduated from the University of Florida and, after those four years of R.O.T.C., was commissioned in the U.S. Army Field Artillery Reserve. In July of that same year he resigned his Army commission to accept appointment as a second lieutenant in the U.S. Marine Corps.

Following Basic School, Lieutenant Chapman served as a battery officer in the 1st Battalion, 10th Marines, at Quantico. In August 1937, he left that regiment to attend the Field Artillery School at Fort Sill, Oklahoma, then rejoined the 10th Marines for duty in San Diego.

Captain Chapman was in the Pacific, commanding the Marine Detachment, USS *Astoria,* when World War II broke out. In June 1942, after seeing action at sea in the battles of the Coral Sea and Midway, Major Chapman was assigned to Marine Corps Schools at Quantico as Executive Officer of the Marine Field Artillery School. By June 1944, Lieutenant Colonel Chapman had returned to the war in the Pacific as Operations Officer of the 11th Marines, and finally as Commanding Officer, 4th Battalion, 11th Marines.

At the end of World War II, after commanding his battalion through the battles of Peleliu and Okinawa, Lieutenant Colonel Chapman returned to the United States. During post-war years he served at Headquarters, Fleet Marine Force, Pacific, and Headquarters Marine Corps in Washington. In 1950, after completing the Senior Course of the Amphibious Warfare School at Quantico, he was assigned as Chief of Supporting Arms Group, Marine Corps Development Center, and promoted to colonel.

From 1952 to 1958, Colonel Chapman commanded the 12th Marines at Camp Pendleton and in Japan; the Marine Barracks, Yokosuka, Japan; and the Marine Barracks, Washington, D.C.

After promotion in 1958, Brigadier General Chapman commanded Force Troops, Fleet Marine Force, Atlantic, until assignment to Headquarters Marine Corps as Assistant Chief of Staff, G-4, and promotion to major general in 1961.

On January 1, 1964, Lieutenant General Chapman was promoted to that rank and named Chief of Staff, Headquarters, Marine Corps. In the summer of 1967, he became Assistant Commandant and on December 4, of that same year, he was nominated for the office of Commandant of the Marine Corps by President Lyndon B. Johnson. On January 1, 1968, General Chapman received his fourth star, and was sworn in as the 24th Commandant of the Marine Corps.

General Chapman's personal decorations include three Navy Distinguished Service Medals; two awards of the Legion of Merit, with Combat "V"; the Bronze Star Medal with Combat "V"; the Navy Commendation Medal with Combat "V"; two awards of the Presidential Unit Citation, the Order of National Security Merit Medal of Korea; and the National Order of Vietnam.

After a four-year term as Commandant, General Chapman retired on December 31, 1971.

Mrs. Chapman is the former Emily Walton Ford, of Birmingham, Alabama. General and Mrs. Chapman have two sons, Leonard F. Chapman, III; and Walton Ford Chapman. Both sons served as Marine infantry officers in the Republic of Vietnam.

ROBERT EVERTON CUSHMAN, JR.

TWENTY-FIFTH COMMANDANT
January 1, 1972

b. St. Paul, Minn., December 24, 1914

GENERAL ROBERT EVERTON CUSHMAN, JR., who earned the Navy Cross during World War II for extraordinary heroism while commanding the 2d Battalion, 9th Marines, during the recapture of Guam, became Commandant of the Marine Corps January 1, 1972.

He attended high school in St. Paul, Minnesota, and was appointed to the U. S. Naval Academy in 1931. Graduating with distinction on June 6, 1935, he was commissioned a Marine second lieutenant.

After completing Marine Officer's Basic School at the Philadelphia Naval Yard, he was ordered to Shanghai, China, where he served as a platoon commander with the 4th Marines, later the 2d Marine Brigade, and received his first campaign ribbon for participation in the defense of the International Settlement during the Sino-Japanese hostilities in 1937.

On his return to the United States in 1938, he served at naval shipyards in Brooklyn, N. Y., and Portsmouth, Va., and was promoted to first lieutenant in August of 1938.

Lieutenant Cushman was next assigned to one of the ceremonial drill units of the Marine Detachment at the New York World's Fair for two years, and was subsequently stationed at Marine Barracks, Quantico, Va., with the Reserve Training Center as G-3 for about 6 months during which all East Coast Reserve Units were put through mobilization training. He was promoted to captain in 1941 and reported aboard the USS *Pennsylvania* as Commanding Officer of the ship's Marine Detachment. While serving in this capacity the Japanese attacked the ship and other naval installations at Pearl Harbor on December 7, 1941.

Upon his transfer from the *Pennsylvania,* he joined the 9th Marines at San Diego as Regimental Adjutant and was later promoted to major and became an infantry Battalion Executive Officer.

Major Cushman made the march from San Diego to Camp Pendleton with his unit in late 1942 and embarked to the Pacific area the following January.

In May 1943, he was promoted to lieutenant colonel and was made Commanding Officer of the 2d Battalion, 9th Marines. He led the battalion into combat for the next two years, earning the Bronze Star Medal with Combat "V" on Bougainville, the Navy Cross during the recapture of Guam, and the Legion of Merit with Combat "V" during the Iwo Jima campaign.

Upon his return to the United States in May 1945, Lieutenant Colonel Cushman was stationed at Marine Corps Schools, Quantico for three years as an instructor and supervisor at the Senior Course of the Amphibious Warfare Schools during the period of evolution of helicopter landing doctrine. Following this, he was named Head of the Amphibious Warfare Branch, Office of Naval Research, in Washington.

Then, from October 1949 until May 1951, he served on the staff of the Central Intelligence Agency. While there he was promoted to colonel in May 1950.

His next duty was with the staff of the Commander in Chief, U. S. Naval Forces, Eastern Atlantic and Mediterranean Fleet, in London, serving as Amphibious Plans Officer for two years, located in London and, later in Naples when the Headquarters moved.

Returning to the United States, he was transferred to Norfolk where he served as a member of the faculty of the Armed Forces Staff College and became Director of the Plans and Operations Division.

Then, in July 1956, he assumed command of the 2d Marines at Camp Lejeune, N. C., and loaded that regiment out to prepare for possible operations during the Suez Canal crisis in 1956. Those operations were not required and the regiment unloaded and returned to Camp Lejeune.

He was then assigned to Washington, D. C., in February 1957, where he served for four years on the staff of Vice President

Richard Nixon as Assistant to the Vice President for National Security Affairs. While serving in this capacity he was promoted to brigadier general in July 1958.

In 1961, Brigadier General Cushman became Assistant Division Commander of the 3d Marine Division on Okinawa and Commander of the Task Force Alfa, a joint command held ready for contingencies. He was promoted to major general in August 1961, and assumed command of the Division.

Following this duty he reported to Headquarters Marine Corps where he was assigned as Assistant Chief of Staff, G-2, and Assistant Chief of Staff, G-3. He served in these capacities for about two years.

Following this, General Cushman was assigned as Commanding General, Marine Corps Base, Camp Pendleton, California, for three years. During this period the Viet Nam war started and all replacements were staged for the Combat units through Camp Pendleton. He was also assigned as Commanding General, 4th Marine Division Headquarters Nucleus. Then, in 1966, he formed the 5th Marine Division and served as its Commanding General until late in the year.

Major General Cushman was then ordered to the Republic of Viet Nam in early 1967, and upon promotion to lieutenant general in June, assumed duty as Commanding General, III Marine Amphibious Force. This became the largest joint combat unit ever led by a Marine in battle, fighting the battles of Khe Sanh and TET '68 among many others. For this, and additional duty as Senior Advisor, I Corps Tactical Zone, and I Corps Coordinator for United States and Free World Military Assistance Forces, General Cushman was awarded two Navy Distinguished Service Medals.

On March 6, 1969, while serving in Viet Nam, General Cushman was nominated by President Richard M. Nixon to be the Deputy Director of the Central Intelligence Agency, in which post he served until named as the Commandant of the Marine Corps. For this duty he was awarded the Distinguished Intelligence Medal.

General and Mrs. Cushman, the former Audrey Boyce of Portsmouth, Va., were married in Portsmouth on January 17, 1940, and have two children, Roberta Lind and Robert E. III.

General Cushman's decorations include: The Navy Cross; three Distinguished Service Medals; Legion of Merit and Bronze Star with Combat "V"; and the Navy Commendation Medal; fourteen foreign decorations; and numerous unit citations and campaign medals.

INDEX

212